SUSTAINABLE
SOCIETY

SUSTAINABLE
SOCIETY

*Making Business, Government
and Money Work Again*

RUDOLF ISLER

Floris Books

Translated by Matthew Barton

First published in German in 2013 by Verlag am Goetheanum, Dornach, Switzerland under the title
Nachhaltigkeit?! Wege aus der Krise durch freie Initiativen

First published in English in 2014 by Floris Books

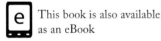 This book is also available as an eBook

British Library CIP Data available
ISBN 978-178250-133-6
Printed in Poland

Contents

Foreword to the English edition

This book was originally written for German-speaking readers. It has been adapted for the English edition.

The book has two chief concerns. Firstly, it highlights the fact that Rudolf Steiner (1861–1925) made significant but far too little-known contributions to the study of economics and sociology, and that his ideas on these subjects have become ever more relevant in recent decades. Secondly it shows that the threefold social organism which he described is not a social theory like many others but has entirely practical applications. This book is therefore based on examples that already exist, that are eminently feasible, and can illustrate key aspects of these ideas.

In European countries people believe that state legislature is primarily responsible for creating laws. But since the law in English-speaking countries is informed by common law and case law, the author hopes that English-speaking readers will more easily understand realities which require Central Europeans to rethink their outlook. This may also be true of some of the practical examples and suggestions offered here. The author also hopes that this book will nurture greater international understanding.

Acknowledgments

For corrections and important suggestions I wish to thank Johanna Wyss, Astrid Lanz, Barbara Isler, Marc Desaules, Daniel Maeder, Gerold Aregger, Urs Ritter. I also want to thank all the people working in farms and schools from whom I learned so much during our shared endeavours.

For the English translation I would like to thank the translator Matthew Barton for his careful formulation of the text, and the editor, Christian Maclean for his many valuable suggestions.

Introduction: Taking heart

The financial crisis at the beginning of the new millennium has shown that we have to completely rethink our monetary system, and part of this book is devoted to that theme. However, the global financial crisis is not an isolated phenomenon. Commerce, working conditions, income levels and the whole education system are currently unsustainable and in equally grave crises, and all kinds of corrective measures have so far met with little success. More than ever today we need to review the whole structure of society and bring detailed insights to bear on it. But the task is so great, and the improvements and innovations needed so universal that the individual, or small groups, with their very limited influence, can lose heart. This is especially true if one thinks the state has to initiate change. As the world is at present, with widespread short-sightedness and pervasive immorality, many people believe that the first step must be to form a political party and enter into the political fray: to change the constitution in a way that obliges all people to act in socially responsible ways. Legislative changes can certainly be important, but they only accompany and reflect a deeper groundswell. In particular, if we no longer expect the state to act in beneficial, social ways, laws ought not to prevent us from taking action ourselves.

We can start such action now and continue every day, for the first steps have already been taken. This book introduces some of these steps, placing them in the overall context of society. When successful they can encourage us, wherever we are, to pursue such things further, developing new forms of company self-administration, the separation of labour from income, new administration of land ownership and capital, and new forms of money. We can see the whole context for such innovation in terms of threefold human co-existence as described in lectures and books by Rudolf Steiner. One aim of this volume is to offer clearer understanding of this threefold idea. But we'll come back to that later.

It is advisable to read through the chapters of this book in order, since they are mutually sustaining and interdependent. For instance, in a chapter on money you may not grasp new methods of money creation as long as you're still caught up in commonly accepted ideas about labour and wages, land ownership and capital. While others have previously said some of the things presented here, there are certain important differences. The author hopes that this book will help give better understanding of the threefold social organism, and that this will feed into living social practice.

1. Money Created in the Economy

1.1 Money's obscure origins

Ever since the financial crises of the twentieth and twenty-first centuries, we have known that the financial world exerts a dominant influence on the real economy and wields ominous power over society. There has been much public debate about reform of the finance sector, and some measures have been implemented. Few people however go as far as to question the very concept and reality of money; and it is not clear that even they have really got to the bottom of the problem.[1] Our modern finance system is so complex, and so obscured by new, ever-multiplying terminology, that only specialists have some hope of grasping it. But they too take quite opposite positions in their disputes, for instance about whether the state should possess sole 'monetative power' – the right to create money – as a fourth distinct right added to the three existing judicial powers of the state, or whether money creation should be left to private banks permitted to take their decisions entirely in accordance with their own profit motives ('free banking').[2] We will examine the degree to which both of these extreme views are partly right and wrong, and therefore inadequate overall.

If we trace the development of money through history, we return to undocumented times. For this reason, many historical accounts rely on deductions and hypotheses, backed up by anthropological observations. In fact, before barter and trade existed, the earliest form of commerce was probably one based solely on gifts, as is still natural within families. A person gave the others what they needed, unconditionally, relying on receiving a gift themselves at some point. Families, clans, tribes and villages procured what they needed by hunting, animal husbandry and farming. As is still the case today in families, there was division of labour, but every member fulfilled their tasks for the others, and received from them what they needed.

Only when people no longer felt an unquestioned sense of belonging with one another did they start to exchange goods. Exchange means that one assigns a value to goods and compares them. The market economy model, originating with Adam Smith in 1776 and later promulgated ever more widely, only holds good from this point of development onwards.[3] However, barter did not begin as most history books say, between people in villages who knew each other well and associated regularly with one another, but between those who rarely met, or did so only once in a lifetime. Thus it applied to trade across larger distances. Traders brought goods from one region to another where they were not available, and in return took back goods that people at home desired. Initially this may simply have involved direct exchange. But as soon as two trading partners could no longer exactly match their needs, they began to use valuable goods, that all knew and could use as a means of exchange, or in other words as money. Shells, silk, precious metals and much else was used in this way. A means of exchange only works if all acknowledge its value. Such acknowledgment can be based on the free agreement of those participating in monetary exchange, or it can be enshrined in law. Money must be 'valid tender'. That is its legal characteristic.

Seeing money's origin in barter makes immediate sense to us, based as it is on the idea that people in ancient times thought as we do now, and desired to be skilful traders. But the further back we go, the less sure we can be that this rational approach is how people actually thought. In ancient Oriental cultures in Mesopotamia and Egypt, people lived in a mythic consciousness and felt their actions to be governed and guided by gods. This was true not only of the kings but of priests who governed a nation by divine authority and administered important aspects of human society – they had water channels and irrigation systems built, and ordained how land was to be allocated. Rather than through barter, goods were supplied and distributed under the governance of temple administrators on behalf of the gods. Money was not needed for this in the sense of a means of exchange, but 'accounts' were required instead to record allocation to every farmer, artisan, and so forth. Numerous such records are still extant in cuneiform tablets dating back to the third millennium BC.

Gold, silver and precious stones belonged to the gods in those days. When kings and queens were adorned with these, they were not showing off their wealth but their affinity with the heavenly world. This is why gold was often placed in a royal grave. An important step in the development of money occurred when people began to desire and seek their own private wealth. The legend of King Midas, who ruled in Lydia in Asia Minor, tells us of this. Midas was so greedy for gold that he wanted everything he touched to turn into it. Dionysus, the god of intoxication, granted him his wish, after which Midas was in danger of starving and dying of thirst since all his food and drink also turned to gold. He recognised that a human being could not use gold for anything, since it had a solely sacramental value. The god took mercy on him and allowed him to wash away his greed for gold in the river Pactolus. Since then, according to the legend, one can find gold in the riverbed. This points us to the fact that money as collateral did not only arise as an innocent means of exchange but from the beginning became associated with greed for earthly riches and power.[4] This is something the proponents of the gold standard ought to reflect on nowadays: that the value of gold does not depend on its value as a commodity but only on our tacit human agreement to regard gold as something valuable, so that it can be used both as a means of exchange and as a capital asset.[5]

1.2 Centrally imposed money

In his book *Debt, the First 5000 Years,* David Graeber demonstrates that markets rarely emerged as places of barter and trade directly from a primary need for barter – as Adam Smith proposed – but that war was (and still is) a much stronger cause for this. Whenever a ruler wished to wage a war, he needed soldiers. After conquest of a foreign land, these soldiers could be provisioned if the conqueror stole treasures of gold and silver from the country's temples and palaces, and turned them into coins embossed with his insignia. He paid his soldiers with this currency, at the same time issuing a decree that the people must pay taxes in the form of these coins. To get hold of this coinage, the people were compelled to sell their goods to the soldiers, thus creating markets. The taxes ensured that the money came back into the ruler's hands in a closed circulation of money. In the medieval period, too, it was in the interest of kings, princes and barons to issue towns with market rights, and militarily defend them. For this purpose they founded cities and accorded their citizens the right to freedom.

From here it was only a small step for the ruling power to ordain that only money that it authorised and issued could be used as means of exchange. Thus began the financial monopoly of political power which holds sway to this day. Rulers often debased the metal content of their coins so that the face value was greater than the commodity value of the metal used. Nevertheless, their subjects had no other choice than to accept these devalued coins in payment. If, on the other hand, the value of the metal used was greater than the face value of the coins, they were hoarded rather than being kept in circulation. The relationship between the face value of coins and the market value of their metal has been a subject of fierce financial and political debate from ancient times through to our own era. The amount of circulating currency and thus its value were always also connected with how much gold and silver could be mined, so that the economy was dependent on the random availability of precious metals. When minting of coins came to be centrally dictated, an epoch arrived in which the value of money was determined by external control, as is still the case today. Nowadays the banking system, consisting of central banks and commercial banks, issues the money it creates to what is called 'introducing new money into the economy'.[6] Is this external regulation of money a prime error in our monetary system?

The development of money did not end with the minting of coins, for coinage was inconvenient when large sums were involved. Traders often had to carry with them heavy loads of coins and precious metals to pay for their purchases, especially if they travelled to foreign lands. Abroad, though, purchasers would evaluate coinage according to its actual value. It was still assumed that the metal of which money was made was a commodity suitable for universal barter. During the long period of history when ordinary money consisted of coins, money was a merchandise. It took a long time before people in the modern era became accustomed to accepting that materially worthless 'things' – such as payment promises, bank receipts, bank notes or bank account figures – could be used as tokens of money.[7] Until about forty years ago, bank notes were only recognised insofar as one could exchange them for gold at any time. Some people are urging a return to the gold standard today, as a way of ensuring that money retains its value. Gold is regarded as a safe asset because it does not devalue. Thus it stands above the transience of all earthly things. Like King Midas, the proponents of gold all have the wealth aspect of gold in view, and still fail to see that one cannot eat and drink gold, and that it offers very little scope indeed for satisfying any other earthly requirements.

As history shows, gold and silver can be stolen. The same is true of bank notes, but not of figures in account books or virtual money. The latter, however, can also be illegally appropriated, as we hear happens on an almost daily basis through financial scams and swindles.

1.3 The three types of money

Before we move on from the history of money to the present day, we need to clarify money's most important attributes. If I give money to someone, I can do so in three different ways.

1) *Purchase money:* I can use money to pay for a commodity or a service. A sale is concluded between a seller and a buyer where the sum of money has the same value as the purchased goods or service. If no right of return or guarantee exists, the purchase money changes hands irrevocably.

2) *Loan money:* If I lend money to someone I do not myself expend it on a purchase but transfer it to the borrower so that *this* person can spend it as purchase money. In other words, the money continues to circulate as purchase money and retains its power of purchase; but something new arises additionally at the same time: a credit-debit relationship between the lender and the borrower that lasts until the debt has been repaid.

3) *Gift money:* If I give a gift of money to someone, I transfer money's power of purchase irrevocably, in the

same way as I do when buying something, but I receive nothing in return.

In his course *World Economy* (CW 340), Steiner pointed out that money is not simply money but that there are three fundamentally different types: purchase money, loan money and gift money. In making this distinction we focus not on its purchasing power – which remains the same for all types, but on the way money is transferred. People enter into diverse mutual relationships through these different types of money.

If I have money in cash or in my bank account, I can expect others to perform services or produce goods for me, which I can purchase. As a lender of credit I have a quite different expectation, which is that the money I lend will be repaid. Here the duration of the credit period is always an important part of the loan agreement. In both cases there is a reciprocal movement: a simultaneous one in the case of purchase, and one at a later date in the case of a loan. When I give money away there is no expectation of reciprocation. The gift is made by a unilateral act of will on the part of the donor. Gifts are often given in return however, and are an important aspect of the system of commerce based on gifts. However, no fixed deadlines are involved for reciprocation. Today by contrast, gifts have largely been replaced by interest-bearing loans, like student loans. A characteristic element of modern capitalism is that it tends to create interest-bearing credit relationships, and tends to give away too little.

Purchase money is short-term money that normally does not remain in one's hands very long but keeps circulating. Loan money, on the other hand, can arise where the flow of money is held up or blocked. If I have acquired more purchase money than I wish to spend on consumption, I can decide not to spend my money but to save it for later instead. In the meantime I make it available to others as a loan, as long as they promise to return it to me at the agreed time.

Loan money therefore occupies an intermediary position between credit and debt, in a tension released once the money is repaid. The third money relationship, that of gift money, has no specified duration. I transfer it immediately and entirely to the recipient. When we buy something we make sure that the service or commodity matches the price we're paying. With a loan, on the other hand, we freely determine the sum: we lend as much as we wish, depending on our individual perception of things. The agreed repayment term must however be strictly adhered to. Gift money is the most generous gesture, and is based solely on my individual perception of a situation.

One can grasp barter and selling with mechanical forms of thought: the seller and the purchaser both desire some gain, and this desire has to be balanced like the two sides of a pair of scales. In loan money and gift money the decisive thing is not this desire but the perception by the lender or giver of another's need. Lending and giving allow something to grow in the medium or long term. In both we are concerned with capacities, though in a quite different way in each case: loan money creates entrepreneurial capital and exists to enable capacities to be *applied* in commerce. Gift money on the other hand exists to create income so that capacities can *grow*. It ensures that those to whom the gift is given have the possibility of living and developing. Thus the three types of money are different in a whole range of ways.

Monetary theory defines money as having three functions: first as a means of exchange, second as a means of storing value, and third as a standard of value. These three functions are poured into one pot and the whole thing is called money. This idea arises because people regard money as

◊ a commodity that is suitable for determining the value of all other commodities;
◊ an easily handled means of exchange;
◊ and an easily stored asset that retains its value.

In fact, only purchase money has the means-of-exchange function, while the value-retaining function is an attribute of loan money. Only the third function (money as standard of value and accounting unit) holds true of all three types of money, and connects them with each other.

Two schools of thought oppose one another here. Ordinary monetary theory starts from money as a thing, and from this abstracts its attributes to arrive at the concept of money.[8] The other approach examines and describes the monetary processes involved in purchasing, lending and giving in ways that allow the nature of money to become ever more apparent. As long as we regard money as something we own we will fail to distinguish between purchase money and loan money. We 'have' both of these: purchase money as liquidity, and loan money as medium or long-term assets. But if we observe the *activity* of money we can see that it is not a 'thing' but a process developing between people and affecting human interactions, and doing so in three fundamentally different ways. In fact, money is nothing other than this monetary relationship between people, and we ought not to look for a material thing underpinning this. This insight into the nature of money is ever more striking in the modern world of finance because only 5 per cent of the money in circulation today consists of actual bank notes or coins. The remaining 95 per cent of existing money (although the amount of this is hugely inflated) is 'book money', figures recorded in accounts: formerly in bank ledgers and today electronically.

It is quite helpful to compare money with water. If we imagine money in the form of coins and bank notes or credit notes, we can follow how these items move from one person's hands to another's, and here we speak of the flow and circulation of money. But the comparison with water shows us something else too, since water moves in two different ways:

◊ We can regard money as a flowing river. Water flows from A to B, then continues to C. Its whole mass moves on from one place to another.

◊ Another image shows money documented by fluctuating bank accounts. There we have a lake with waves. In one place a trough arises between waves, matched elsewhere by a wave crest. The wave troughs are as deep as the wave crests are high: both fluctuate around a mean level which is that of the water at rest. Only the wave forms move from A to B and then C, while the water as mass and 'thing' stays where it is, merely rising and falling.

It is not too difficult to imagine that money is like flowing water, but the second metaphor makes greater demands on the flexibility of our thinking. It can help us, however, to move away from the concept of money as a thing. The wave movements of fluctuating accounts are more difficult to grasp since the movements involved there are not of things but of relationships, and reveal something of the mystery of money. Important experts in the field such as Hans Christoph Binswanger and Bernard Lietaer have found it necessary to draw on fairytale and archetypal images in their efforts to describe and explain money.[9]

1.4 Money creation today

Cash consists of bank notes and coins, and only these are held to be legal tender. The state holds a monopoly on their production. The minting of coins is directly subject to the state treasury, and the state commissions the national central bank to issue them. When people want to sell something they are obliged to accept this money within the state's area of jurisdiction (though coins may only be accepted up to a specific amount: in Europe up to 50 euros irrespective of the purchase sum). Bank account transfers or cheques on the other hand are not a statutory means of payment. When I open a bank account, however, I declare my agreement to accept this form of money. Any bank client can ask for his money to be paid out to him in cash. Usually people do this only to a limited degree, and therefore a bank will only hold small quantities of bank notes and coins. If the bank customer does not insist on drawing money cash in bank notes, the bank credits the sum required as bank money to a bank account.

Now the golden rule of banking states that long-term credit must be funded by long-term assets, whereas capital received for a short term may only be lent in the short term. For a long time now the banks have no longer fully adhered to this rule since they found that the customers whose money they hold never redeem the full sum of their deposits within the agreed withdrawal period. Therefore banks can use these demand deposits (site deposits), which customers can demand back at any time, for making further loans, even longer-term ones, or use them for speculative purposes. If I have a sum of money in my bank account this money is not sitting in the bank waiting for me until I need it again. The bank goes about its business by offering credit to others or engaging in speculative transactions on the stock market or in foreign currency trading. In this way banks turn short-term into long-term money, and this 'rescheduling' is an important aspect of their business activities today. Returning to the terms we set out above, we can say that in its credit business the bank, without asking for our agreement, passes on our purchase money to others. Purchase money and loan money are therefore not separated by clear rules but flow into one another.

To secure its credit, the bank requires its borrowers to cede property rights (mortgages and other credit securities). For its transactions the bank not only uses its customers' deposits but can also procure liquid assets from the central bank, in the form of either bank notes or bank money. The central bank in turn demands security for this in the form of bonds with legally defined attributes. The central bank always makes enough money available to the corporate banks as is needed for monetary transactions. But the banks will only take as much central bank money as they absolutely need, since they have to pay interest on it.

Central banks can also directly intervene in the securities market (the open market) by buying up shares and bonds. In the USA a great proportion of money is created in the Federal Reserve system (Fed) by corporate banks buying up treasury bonds. This central bank money, which enables the American government to maintain its liquidity, attracts interest since the government promises interest to the holders of treasury bonds. In 1971, during the Vietnam war, the convertibility of the dollar to gold was cancelled, and other currencies followed suit shortly afterwards. Since then, this type of money creation is dictated only by the upper limit of debt which the United States government imposes on itself, a level it continually pushes upwards. Over 75 per cent of all the world's money is dollars, and 80 per cent of these dollars are elsewhere than America, in countries where central banks hold them as currency reserves. This basically means that the currencies of other countries are dependent on the dollar or in other words on the American state's increasing debts.

Without examining all aspects of money creation we can say that nowadays all money is created as loan money and only enters purchase-money circulation as means of payment at a second stage. The bank system, headed by the central bank, introduces all money into circulation via credit. Today money always originates in someone's debts, rather than through the creation of economic values. It is conjured forth from nothing, and it is therefore called 'fiat money' by analogy with the biblical expression in Latin, *fiat lux* (let there be light). Money thus created only remains in circulation as long as the debt lasts. When the debtor repays his debt to the banking system, he inevitably withdraws the sum from purchase-money circulation. In this way the banks have the possibility, within this system, of creating money and destroying it again.

Loan money creation is today assuming ever more huge dimensions since ever more money is used in the rapid increase of money assets. Liquid money or purchase money is needed for money speculation: speculators can borrow this from the banks but then, instead of passing it on, they hoard it so as to have it to hand for their speculative trading. Money has detached itself increasingly from the real economy. By means of speculative funds, growing amounts of money can be made – and often also lost again. Every gain by one person is balanced by another's loss. This redistribution of money leads to an ever-increasing gulf between wealth and poverty. Four billion dollars of purchase money are used every 24 hours in the speculative foreign currency trade, and vast profits are made. The losers, ultimately, are people in the real economy.

If we study the Asian crisis of 1997 we can see how flourishing national economies can be destroyed by targeted currency transactions. The large amount of fluid money needed for currency and derivatives trading is willingly created as loan money 'from nothing' by the banking system under the direction of the central bank. Another absurd consequence of modern money creation is that private capital owners earn money from the debts of many nations. This is also true in the case of the much-praised 'emergency bail-out funds', which supposedly protect over-indebted nations in Europe from bankruptcy. Here again the great amount of extra funds needed are created by the banks and made available as loan money to the IMF and the EU. The banks and the owners of private capital rake in the profits in the form of interest.

1.5 The security of money created by banks

Always implicit in loan money is the question of whether one can be sure of repayment and interest payments. When banks grant credit, they check the borrower's productivity to see if they are likely to have sufficient income in future to service the debt. They also require the borrower to pledge assets as security. This second type of security can lead banks not to check the borrower's productivity carefully enough, as was seen in the American mortgage crisis of 2007. Even mortgages do not give absolute security, especially where a property is mortgaged right up to the limit of its market value. When real estate prices in the US did not rise in the way people had come to expect over decades, but fell, many mortgages were no longer adequately secured. The banks' mortgage assets lost their value. But the banks had already passed on these assets by packaging them in 'structured bonds' and selling them to Europe. Thus the American mortgage crisis also dragged European banks into its vortex, necessitating 'bail-out' measures by governments.

The central banks also require securities for the loan money they make available to the private banks. If the banks own shares they can surrender them to the central bank in order to obtain money. Other assets offering security for funds loaned by the central bank are gold reserves, foreign currency and government bonds. Both the central banks and the corporate banks create money without creating real values at the same time in the form of goods or services. In their balance sheets they set this money against government debts, mortgages and shares, which are not goods but marketable property rights. The property rights to land and means of production are traded on the property and bonds market, where prices are highly reliant on financial speculation. Thus money depends on this and on government debts. But as we will explain later, in ideas of social threefolding it becomes important to entirely overcome the purchasibility of land and the means of production.

What does it mean if, for instance, the European central bank lists dollar stocks in its balance sheet as assets, and if the Swiss National Bank does the same with euros and dollars? Swiss francs and euros are partly reliant on the dollar, and the dollar in turn is founded to a considerable degree on the debts of the US State. National debts, however, are something fundamentally dubious. Modern states are not in the main productive corporations that increase their productivity with the aid of credit. Instead they fund social expenditure, military armaments, schools, universities, etc. From an economic perspective, none of this is commercially productive but belongs to consumption. State debts can therefore only be repaid from taxation. All these questionable and to some extent absurd circumstances are, as will become increasingly clear, connected with the fact that we assign economic tasks, including money management, to government administrations.

1.6 Complementary currencies

Could there be a form of money which the economy does not receive from an alien source but that *we* ourselves create in the course of our economic activity? In the 1980s local and regional alternative money systems developed in several countries suffering high unemployment. They do not replace state money but complement it. Over four thousand complementary currencies now exist in the world. One especially interesting type of such currency is the following: unemployed people with no money but much available time, offer each other reciprocal services and charge for these through a billing point that they communally establish. Drawing on the example of Time

Dollars, which started up in 1986, Bernard A. Lietaer describes how this works:

> Joe no longer sees very well and therefore can't drive. But he needs a new pair of specialised shoes that can only be obtained from the other end of town. Julia offers to drive the one-hour journey and collects the new shoes. For this she receives a one-hour credit, while Joe owes one hour. Julia can use her credit to buy biscuits baked by a neighbour of hers, while Joe pays back what he owes by working in a community garden, or undertaking some other activity not prevented by his weak eyesight. If Joe did an hour's work in Julia's garden this would be a simple exchange. But Joe can equally work in a different garden to balance his account, and then Julia can use her credit to buy those biscuits ... Joe and Julia do not need to match their needs and services to each other. For this reason, Time Dollars are ... real money: an agreement within a community to use something (in this case labour hours) as a means of exchange. In other words, Joe and Julia have created money.[10]

Such systems are known as LETS (Local Exchange Trading Systems). The exchange communities usually employ labour hours as a calculation unit and call this by names such as Time Dollars or Green Dollars. In Japan, since care of the sick and elderly has become unaffordable, 'nursing currencies' have arisen in many places. This voluntary care is likewise calculated in labour hours. International barter trade has also increased greatly in the last thirty years, and plays a role in national trade too. It uses an important accounting currency whereby the supply of goods is charged for via a clearing office without the use of legally valid tender. While international barter trade is mostly conducted in US dollars, this is only a calculation unit and does not play any part in dollar circulation. Around a quarter of world trade takes place as barter trading.

In 1944 John Maynard Keynes, as Britain's representative at Bretton Woods, proposed the same principle for the International Clearing Union operating between national currencies. The idea was that government central banks should be members of this clearing system, each of them running an account with a fixed maximum debt limit based on each country's annual exports and imports. Keynes suggested a new currency as accounting unit, which he called Bancor. His proposals came to nothing since the USA wanted to make the dollar into the leading global currency, and was able to do so as the greatest world power. A world currency such as Bancor, by contrast, would have required no leading power or even global government, nor would it have served any such dominance. According to Keynes's proposals, Bancor would not have been a general currency but would only have served to balance payments between central banks.[11]

1.7 Money as clearing system

The history of these monetary accounting systems is highly significant if we want the economic life we all participate in to create its own, autonomous management and stewardship. Rudolf Steiner said a good deal about this kind of independent administration of economic life, though made no specific comments about a new monetary system. But in his innovative book, *Towards Social Renewal,* he suggests that we should

> ... direct our attention to the distinctive nature
> of social institutions that will be needed if the
> threefold social order is to be realised. For example,
> here a national government will no longer be

obliged to endorse money as legal tender but such endorsement will depend on measures issuing from the administrative bodies running the economy. You see, in a healthy social organism money can be nothing other than a remittance for commodities produced by others, which we can draw from the whole realm of economic life by virtue of the fact that we ourselves have produced goods and released them into this realm. Through money circulation an economic domain becomes a unified economy. Via the whole life of the economy, each person produces something for others, whereas within an economic domain one is concerned only with commodity values.[12]

These are vital insights. On 30 May 1919 Steiner adds these further comments:

> ... the characteristic money has currently acquired – of being a commodity – will fall away. The monetary system will consist only of a kind of adaptable accounting system to record the exchange of goods between those who belong to each economic area. There will be a kind of credit recording system when someone procures something he needs. Thus the monetary system will be a kind of accounting system, a flexible, fluctuating one.[13]

In Steiner's day his comments could only be understood as meaning that money, which largely consisted of bank notes back then, must be reinterpreted conceptually as 'adaptable accounting'. It is easier for us today because most money is indeed recorded as book money. Still more important is the existence now, on a small scale, of the monetary systems described above, which have arisen as purely 'recorded accounts relating to the exchange of goods'. We can therefore base our understanding on practical experiences in this field rather than intellectual constructs, and can reflect on what is actually involved here.

The complementary currencies described are book money created within a community of equally entitled members, always in the precise amounts needed for payments. The members of the monetary community form voluntary associations and make contractual agreements to report their sales and purchases to a clearing house. There an account exists for each participant, household and company, starting with zero, since to begin with no money exists that can first be paid in. At least, this will be the case if money arises solely from real economic activity by the members who sell to and purchase from each other. It is also necessary to choose a unit of value and agree this contractually – for instance, the value resulting from one working hour. This standard of value gives rise to all prices of goods and services. Other standards of value are also conceivable, and, as we will see, useful.

Credit is recorded on the account of a member who sells goods or services to another, and a debt of equal amount is lodged on the account of the purchaser. Participants in the monetary system expect that anyone acquiring a debit note will likewise perform an economic service so that the debt on their account is rebalanced. It is possible to ask in advance for proof that this will be done. Likewise, someone who receives a credit can use it to purchase goods or services from another association member. Thus every account fluctuates around the zero point between debit and credit. This is similar to the way we ordinarily cover our monthly expenses with our monthly wage, so that during the month our current account fluctuates around an average level.

No one should accrue more debts than they can regularly pay off. Nor does it make sense here to have a credit that is not regularly used. It is therefore necessary for every account to have a lower debt limit and an upper credit limit. The community itself will determine what these levels are by adopting agreed rules. If increasing productivity means that incomes and therefore general prosperity increase, the upper and lower limits on purchase money accounts can be extended by agreement. In this case the potential (not the actual) amount of money in the system is enlarged. The purchase money account limits for companies is determined by their regular weekly, monthly or quarterly turnover. Sums in excess of these limits, whether in the red or the black, will be regarded as loan money, separated from purchase money and transferred to loan accounts. Credit on loan money accounts will then be subject to 'ageing' or depreciation of the loan money. Debts will be covered by a credit agreement with a specific duration and, if desired, an interest rate.[14]

Although we speak of debits and credits on purchase money accounts, this is not loan money. What is the difference? Loaned money is something I must repay to those who made it available to me, whereas purchase money involves credits and debits towards the whole monetary community. These are not paid back in money but balanced through the provision of goods and services, which embody the nature of purchase money. Already in our present system my money – even the cash in my pocket – is a credit held by me against all who acknowledge this money and are willing to sell me something in return for it. The words 'credit' or 'asset' should not mislead us into thinking it is something one 'owns'. It would be better described as a claim or right to goods and services; and instead of debts, one could speak of an 'obligation to perform' as far as purchase money is concerned.[15]

Basically, all money consists of alternating credit and debit. In the case of purchase money these positions relate to the whole monetary community from which I can draw services or goods, and to which I likewise owe these. In the case of loan money on the other hand, the debt relates to the credit-giver to whom I must repay what I have borrowed.[16] If someone spends money but does nothing for others, this harms the community since purchase money available to the individual originates with the community not with a bank. This is not true of 'pure consumers' who live from gift money and are not obliged to engage in economic activities, but can only spend as much money as they receive in gifts.

In the modern history of money, book money was originally derived from cash. In seeking the archetype of money the sequence must be reversed: money displays its intrinsic nature as book money, that is, as a balancing of accounts. Secondary to this we can create paper money and coins as monetary tokens. Anyone who has a bank account can ask to receive such tokens, whereupon the corresponding sum is debited from his account. Today, most payments are undertaken without cash; but in many situations paper money is a useful means of payment. Since money consists of relationships between people, the monetary system is largely reliant on means of communication, and this becomes more or less apparent depending on the communication method. In regard to modern electronic forms of communication, we can say that it is high time we allowed money, in accordance with its intrinsic nature, to arise as book money, that is, as the book-keeping of purchase money. Loan money then arises from purchase money through a secondary process which we will examine in the next section.

The social order must make liquid money available to everyone – which means giving each person the possibility of spending money. Money circulation must start from this rather than from the idea that someone 'owns' money. This is expressed in the fact that purchase money accounts start at zero and oscillate between plus and minus balances.

1.8 Ageing money

Like his contemporary Silvio Gesell, Rudolf Steiner stated that money is in unreal competition with real goods which degrade at various rates and lose their value. The money we possess, by contrast, retains its value. For this reason Silvio Gesell urged that money should similarly continuously decline in value by imposing a negative interest on it. He called this 'depreciative money'. Steiner partly adopted this point of view but, because he distinguished between the three types of money, said that purchase money retains its value. He spoke of the 'ageing of money'. To age means to come closer to death. After a certain period, he said, money should 'die' just as living creatures do, or like machines that break down. If one does not treat money in accordance with these laws of life, he says, it goes rampant. Money needs to be tamed. Explaining this in his lectures on World Economy in 1922, he said:

> Now you may say: That is just a scheme. No, it is nothing of the sort. What I have just explained to you is the actual reality. That is how the economic process actually wills it. The economic process of its own accord makes the money grow old. The fact is that it does not appear to grow old – the fact that we still buy things with 1910 money in the year 1940 is only a mask. In doing so we do not really buy with this money; we buy with a fictitious money-value. If you tame money, if you really assign to it a certain age, letting young money – as loan-money – be more valuable than the old, then you will be impressing the money with its real effective value, the value it possesses through its position in the economic process. This value really only inheres in the money insofar as it is loan-money, for even if money is loan-money, as purchase money it still retains its former value.[17]

In line with this last sentence, we can recognise that wherever Steiner speaks about *money* in the above quotation, in relation to the ageing and taming of money, we must understand *loan money*.

The distinction between purchase money, loan money and gift money which Rudolf Steiner introduced is the vital difference between his view and the theory of depreciating money. Of all the theorists commenting on our current financial and economic crisis, adherents of Silvio Gesell and his 'natural economic order' are among the best we have today, but they lack this distinction between the different types of money.[18] In the way they formulate their ideas one can see that they picture money as a 'thing', that is, as bank notes (money tokens on paper). Thus money is merely 'money' for them, and they assign depreciation indiscriminately to all of it.

In the case of complementary currencies this can function perfectly well too. The theory of depreciating money states that diminishing value is necessary to prevent money hoarding. This 'circulatory assurance' is necessary, they say, especially if one wishes to get rid of interest and compound interest. This argument shows that the problem focused on here only arises when money accumulates; or in other words at the transition point between purchase money and loan money.[19] The money we have today could only become subject to depreciation of value by external measures imposed on it, enforced by state legislation. But if the state or central bank were to impose this depreciation on the loan money they create, all money would diminish in value, including purchase money. This is also the case with the Chiemgauer currency which the Chiemgauer administrators create and bring into circulation at a price in euros. There is an important difference however: through taxation the state would take possession of the difference arising through value loss. In the case of the Chiemgauer currency, individuals can themselves determine whom these sums should benefit in the form of gift money.

Now Steiner said that money should not have ageing externally imposed upon it. This is because the economic process itself seeks to give this attribute to loan money, to which a specific term or period is always attached. Clearly this is so when money arises as purchase money in the economic process. If our theory of money starts from book money, or in other words from cash-less clearing systems, the payment process does not appear to us in the guise of money that passes as a tangible thing from the purchaser to the vendor. Instead, the purchaser's assets in relation to the whole money community are reduced by the amount of the purchase price, and at the same time a new vendor asset arises in relation to this money community. Purchase money always arises as something new, and no time factor attaches to it as to loan money. Money only acquires a time attribute when it is accumulated as capital, both when it is hoarded and when given to others as credit for a specified period.

When we speak of ageing money we mean all kinds of assets, which we can sum up as loan money. This shows why Steiner said that his proposals were not a scheme but an actual attribute of money within the economic process. Ageing here means simply that it is subject to time conditions, and ultimately will come to an end. For this reason Steiner's phrase, 'ageing of money' means something very different from 'depreciative' money. Ageing is a term that can be applied not only to living creatures but also to the things we use. For instance, a car may remain useful for twenty years or so, albeit with increasing repair costs; the moment it breaks down and is no longer worth repairing can occur very suddenly.

If money arises as purchase money, loan money can always develop from it if someone does not spend it but saves it instead, and so accumulates money that is hoarded and thus withdrawn from circulation. The hoarded money is like a blockage in circulation. It comes back into flow as purchase money when passed on as a loan, as long as the borrower spends this money as purchase money. But the blockage remains with the creditor as capital and reserve. In this case too, therefore, we can say that purchase money retains its value. But as regards hoarded money and loan money we must urge an ageing process due to its relation to time. How old should loan money grow to be? Steiner cited a period of between fifteen and thirty years, though stated these were only an illustration, to give a rough idea. In general, and theoretically, all we can say about the ageing of loan money is that we must compare it with the ageing of investment assets (machines, vehicles, buildings). These reach very different ages. Perhaps we could assign an average age to loan money, though this could not be scientifically specified: it would be a matter for the money community to regulate, keeping in mind all the factors relating to the life expectancy of loan money (that is, capital assets).

If money is handled in this way, an ageing money asset that is not needed as purchase money during its life-span will eventually lose its purchase money value for the previous owner, and can then only be given away. A statement such as this triggers alarm today, since in our current social order we rely on capital assets for our pensions. Other measures need to be put in place to cover this, for it is only our mistaken monetary system that gives us the illusion that, in thirty, forty or fifty years' time, we will live off the capital that we are saving today. In economic reality we can only live in our old age from the labour and productivity of younger, still active people. Pensions therefore belong under distribution of economic net income, as we will describe in Chapter 2.

By its very nature a loan must be repaid. Today however there are also loans with no regular repayment requirement, or ones that can repeatedly be renewed because they are regarded as secured by property or land. Such mortgage securities must be removed from corporate loans (see Chapters 3 & 4). Property security does not depend on economic processes but on property rights which are put into play when mortgaged. If there is no property security, loan money is intrinsically connected with depreciation. The borrower can easily recognise this since the means of production he bought with loan money gradually lose their value. It is not so easy for the lender to see that his assets must be similarly affected. These assets, however, lose their useful task in the economy if they are seen as of unlimited duration, and continue to be used as loan money in perpetuity. After a certain period they must be given away as gift money. Due to our modern view of property, we regard the writing off of assets as expropriation. But since this is economically useful and necessary, the concept of ownership must change so that an asset allowing us to benefit from the economic productivity of others must be of limited duration.

There are two conceivable technical solutions for the depreciation of assets. They can either be marked down in regular ratios or alternatively they can lose their entire value at the end of a specified life-span. Silvio Gesell proposed gradual, regular depreciation. With book money this can be done on a precise, daily basis. Rudolf Steiner preferred a different method, well-suited for bank notes – which accounted for a much greater proportion of money at the beginning of the twentieth century than they do today. Steiner suggested printing an expiry date on bank notes. Money with an expiry date is of lower value as loan money towards the end of its validity since it can only be lent on a short-term basis and therefore will bear only a small amount of interest. With book money it is not so straightforward to assign a duration to sums of money. Both technical measures therefore make sense, one that applies to book money, the other to bank notes. They will ensure

1. MONEY CREATED IN THE ECONOMY

that the compound interest effect ceases, and that an asset is eventually transformed into a gift and disappears.

Both methods of money depreciation can be used alongside each other. For long-term funds stored on capital accounts, a monetary community can determine rules applied by the clearing house for ongoing depreciation. When an asset is paid out as paper money, the year of issue and expiry can be printed on it. We are, after all, already used to expiry dates on perishable goods. After expiry of their validity, the paper money could only be returned to the clearing bank as gift money. If the notes were returned prior to this, the clearing centre would separate from the funds the depreciation amount due as gift money. Thus bank notes would always lose value irrespective of whether they were used as purchase or loan money. This disadvantages paper money, and precisely by this means would make money laundering more difficult. The successful Chiemgauer regional currency shows that something like this can work, and is happily accepted by participants in the economy. (The Chiemgauer currency is an outstanding illustration, even though this complementary money does not originate in the economy in a primary way, but is based on the euro, since you have to use euros to buy Chiemgauers.)

The owner of assets can give away the write-off sums to institutions working in the social and cultural domain. The purpose or aim of the gift can be specified by the person from whose capital the assets come, who can seek advice on this. The latter can also conclude an agreement with the company to whom funds have been lent in which both parties together determine which institution the repaid loan should be given to. When gift money arrives in the account of a gift recipient or institution, it becomes purchase money for the latter.

Credit is usually given to improve productivity in the economy. When the credit is repaid, the repayment originates in the additional productivity facilitated by the credit. This increased productivity has not been achieved by the lender, but by cultural or spiritual activities – that is, through education and invention. We can therefore see that spiritual or cultural life has a justified claim to the yield of this increased productivity. If repayment of credit occurs, in line with ageing of loan money, as gift to training and research institutions, the latter acquire the means to continue their work.

Money arising as book money in clearing systems acquires attributes that allow it to turn from purchase money into loan money and then to gift money in an unforced, smooth and economically useful way.

1.9 Interest – a good thing or not?

Someone who saves money and passes on what he has saved in the form of a loan relinquishes the money's liquidity for a certain period. He can be paid for this relinquishment by means of interest. Interest is however morally debatable. The three great religions based on the Old Testament long ago forbade interest charges (Exod.22:25, Deut.23:20). The prohibition still exists in modern Islam. However, a distinction was made as to whether funds were lent to clansmen and fellow believers or to foreigners. In the first case it was assumed that the loans were consumer credit used to help friends in a difficult situation. In the latter case, on the other hand, they were regarded as production loans through which one would be participating in some business that would hopefully bring good yields; and here, therefore, interest was tolerated.

Interest is thought to be especially harmful when added to one's assets to create compound interest. Economics however assigns an important function to interest: it is thought to encourage those who have accumulated assets not to hoard their money but make it available to the economy as a loan. In this way it is not withdrawn from general circulation. The theory of depreciative money states that ongoing decrease in value or 'discounting' of the money ensures circulation. But in the case of accrued assets, this only works if money given as loans is not subject to discounting. This alone makes it an interesting proposition to give credit. This can be achieved simply by the borrower agreeing to repay the full sum to the lender, thus maintaining the full amount of his assets. In fact this is nothing other than an application of interest at a level high enough to compensate for the discounting or depreciation. The assets do not increase, it is true, but ageing of the loan money is, for all practical purposes, rescinded. Interest retains the function of ensuring money stays in circulation but is rendered innocuous through capital depreciation. Udo Herrmannstorfer calls this process 'dynamically sustained monetary stability'.[20]

Steiner rejected a prohibition on interest, and attracted some debate and criticism in consequence, since interest can clearly do harm. It only does so, though, if interest is too high, and is used to increase capital assets – that is, when compound interest is created. Steiner strictly rejected compound interest. In *Towards Social Renewal,* he relates the question of interest to the process whereby money 'wears out' so that one receives ever less interest for it as time continues.[21] In a discussion he said:

> If you quote what I said on interest, please remember that in every sentence of my book I sought to describe honestly the real state of affairs, and that I strictly rejected anything that amounts to compound interest. If the reality I describe in my book really came about then growth of capital as occurs today, in which a capital can double in fifteen years, would be out of the question. I was

not speaking of such things but of legitimate interest ... it has to become possible for previous work to be used for later productivity. However, the only way that this can happen, the only way ... for me to have a certain benefit from this ... is by means of legitimate interest, as I call it ...[22]

In *World Economy*, he said that if one pays no interest on a loan then one feels an obligation in return to lend to the other when needed. If one does pay interest, on the other hand, the obligations have been met in a different way. We might add if I receive goods from someone, I also feel under an obligation to give something in return; or I can redeem the obligation by paying a price for the goods. In the first instance we apply principles of the gift economy, and in the second that of calculated exchange.

Interest should be seen as the price of someone's labour and thus as purchase money. Compound interest, on the other hand, increases loan money. If one wishes to avoid the latter, interest must remain within modest limits. It must cover actual costs, especially those of administering the loan and the risk that it may not be repaid; and in addition facilitate a small net income. The asset is gradually transformed into gifts through depreciation (discounting). Interest on the other hand works by giving one a useable yield from former work. After all, we cannot consume something old and previously accumulated but only the product of a current, new economic action. From this perspective, rules could be laid down for interest rates to ensure that the level of interest is not determined by the capital market as it is today.

Nowadays, one of the tasks of central banks is to affect interest rates. Steiner believed that the rate should be determined by the 'rights state'.[23] But since modern governments are very imperfect 'rights states', internal interest rules can initially be agreed by monetary communities. The monetary community will decide here whether interest should be compensation for asset depreciation or not. Whether the interest should be equal in value to the discounting cannot be determined in a logical, abstract way; instead, a general sense of justice can gradually develop through the contractual regulations in this new realm.

1.10 Can new money be created as loan money?

The enormous developments in commerce that have arisen since the Industrial Revolution required large amounts of capital investment in production facilities. Adequate sums for this were available in countries like England through their colonial trading. Modern economic theory states that new, additional money has to enter the economy in the form of credit. If this were distributed directly to consumers, the increased demand for goods would lead to price increases and money devaluation, and thus inflation. Therefore additional means of production first needs to be created, and only when more consumer goods could be produced in consequence, is it acceptable for consumer demand to increase.

But the creation of loan money, if this arises 'from nothing', does have an inflationary effect. When the companies that receive more credit purchase more production facilities, the prices of the latter rise. Machine factories and building corporations employ additional labour forces, or their employees work overtime so that their incomes increase. Thus the quantity of money expands before the new production facilities have been finished and come into use. There is a delay before new consumer goods come onto the market, and this delay has an inflationary action. We do not necessarily perceive this because nowadays factors are at work that counteract the rise in prices. The required additional goods can be imported, and here the exchange rate comes into play. Nowadays, foodstuffs and raw materials are requisitioned from poor countries at low prices. The internal economy of a country, under pressure from cheap imports, is kept going by means of subsidies. These factors will remain in force while there are national economies with borders between 'home' and 'abroad', national currencies, and imports and exports.

In the last four lectures of *World Economy*, Rudolf Steiner strongly emphasised the need to distinguish between a national economy and the global economy. Things will gradually change as the more or less separate national economies transform into one self-contained global economy without external borders. Customs at national borders and imbalances in the exchange rates between currencies affect prices in a complex way, and thus the value of money too. In the corporate finance world that has become an end in itself, large amounts of the loan money today created by the banks vanish in speculative trading with money. All these occurrences must be taken into account if we are to form a clear, detailed picture in each instance of whether loan money creation has an inflationary effect.

There is no inflationary effect if the amount of money that people have available for purchase is equal to overall productivity. However, this state of equilibrium must not be created by monetary policies, but develops by itself if money arises only as purchase money, and only within the economic process. Even as purchase money it should not be introduced into the economy from without, as would be the case if, for example, a central bank were to distribute to all individuals as much money as they needed. A central bank of this kind would not have arisen from the economic process but would be a state or state-related institution governing all the people of a particular national jurisdiction (or the whole world) on an equal basis.

Loan money has the fundamental attribute of being made

available by one person or body to another. As far as the recipient is concerned, it is always externally determined. This must not be the case with money creation. We saw in Section 1.5 that modern loan money creation is based on national debts, on the trade with means of production (shares) and on land ownership. If states do not accrue debts, and means of production are not traded, loan money creation becomes impossible. Without loan money creation, the quantities of money needed for the speculative trade in foreign currencies and derivatives would not exist. Here we see that monetary questions are closely related to other social questions that will be considered later.

Loan money is of great importance as corporate capital. But how do entrepreneurs get hold of the capital that they need? In a closed economic region this is only possible if we do not use the economy's whole net yield, distributed as income, in order to purchase consumer goods. If we did this, the whole product of the economy would be used up. Loan money is only available if some of the income is put aside as savings. Then parts of the economic product remain free and can be used to manufacture production facilities. By its very nature, money is an abstract thing, and can detach itself from tangible economic values with which it is directly connected as purchase money. In this way it can become loan capital, giving entrepreneurs the opportunity to use their inventive (spiritual) capacities in way useful for the economy. In *World Economy*, Steiner says that the abstract nature of money means that 'money becomes ... the instrument, the medium for the Spirit to enter into the economic organism in the division of labour.'[24]

There is no need to ask whether saved capital will be sufficient for the large capital requirements of corporations, since in the self-contained global economy there *is* no other source for funding the means of production. We can assume that if all people were allocated an equal income, then all would have sufficient opportunity to save money, and either lend this or give it away. Both these latter forms of money are necessary for a vibrant economy: loan money for corporate development, and gift money for the training and education of human skills and capacities.

1.11 The value of money

Every sum of money consists of a number and a unit of value, by means of which the value of commercial goods can be determined. But money also has an intrinsic value which arises from the price of goods and services offered, whose value is measured in terms of money. When goods become more expensive, the value of money – also called 'purchase power' – falls. It is not easy to determine the value of money if, in this reciprocal relationship between money and goods, all prices are equally justified. Throughout history, therefore, people have repeatedly favoured specific values, such as gold or, in the recent past, the dollar. They thought they were clearer about where they stood because of gold's reference value. In the community currencies of exchange circles, one hour's labour is often used as the unit of value. This makes sense for them because the main exchange in these communities is of services. This is also possible for the exchange of goods, however, since one can say that if someone works 40 hours a week, he and his family have to be able to live from the yield of his work. (If only what is really necessary were produced, 20 hours a week would be more than enough.)

Money is only a measure of value if we know how many essential goods it can buy. The value of money cannot be defined in terms of gold therefore, since gold is not essential to survival and only has value by virtue of allowing us to buy something useful with it. It is common to measure the value of money against a 'supermarket trolley' of goods thought to meet average human needs. This certainly relates to our basic need for food, clothing and habitation, but all 'normal' needs are also often included, such as sickness costs, insurance, water and electricity, information, travel, leisure activities, etc. A 'price index' is calculated from these 'necessities', and monetary policy is supposed to track this. But what is the most meaningful reference value for money? Should we not think first and foremost of food, of our 'daily bread'? Food is the foundation of all economic activity. If we have food, then we can do something else afterwards; without it, all productivity ceases. In bygone eras when we still all took care of our own needs, we did not yet need money. But as soon as we no longer provided our own food, but relied on the labour of others for this, we had to relate the value of our work to that of food. The yield of our labour must be sufficient to exchange it for food. This reference value holds good however extensive and complex the economy becomes.

Rudolf Steiner proposed using grain as money's measure of value. Here grain represents our daily food and at the same time all agricultural products. Grain money has been a currency in the past. In Mesopotamia, barley was the most ancient unit of value, to which copper and silver were added later. One *gur* of barley (a sack?) was seen as equal in value to one shekel of silver (around 8 grams?). Until some time in the nineteenth century, taxes and basic interest were stipulated in grain measures. The German agronomist, Albrecht Thaer (1752–1828), as well as his students estimated agricultural output in rye units.

During the runaway inflation in Germany in the 1920s, there were ideas of using rye as a standard of value and general currency. This idea was dropped when the Rentenmark was introduced in 1923.

Insofar as money is a standard of value it must be standardised like any other measure. To do so, it must basically be calibrated against goods and services. Money could be standardised against grain. Steiner described this very vividly, saying that paper money could bear a figure stating how much wheat it was equal to. This would result in the price of grain in this currency always remaining constant. The prices of other agricultural produce could still fluctuate, thus giving stimulus for production adjustments within agriculture. But overall the prices of foodstuffs would remain stable, and farmers would not – as they do today – suffer from increasing price pressures. All other prices would arise through their relation to the price of grain. One hour's labour also acquires its value within this pricing context. Even if grain is chosen as a measure of money's value, the price for one hour's labour remains an important factor, not just in the services sector but also in trade. But one always has to remember that payment is not made for the hour of work itself, but for whatever is produced during one hour's labour.

Defining the value of money through the performance of one hour's labour is abstract and general; it only becomes tangible and specific when we establish what essential goods and services can be produced in one hour. Here, therefore, we come back to indispensible economic products that we gain from nature: to food, textile fibres for our clothes and building materials for our houses.

To understand grain money we can picture the following: in an economy that does not as yet have money, a farmer gives another person a kilogram of grain and receives for it a note on which is written: 'value: 1 kg grain.' This credit note can enter circulation when other people recognise and accept it; and it is nothing other than a book entry in a generally recognised monetary accounting system. The value of money in fact always depends on it being generally and uniformly acknowledged. This is a question of the law that can be created through contractual agreements within monetary communities. If I wish to purchase something with 'grain money', I don't have to carry sacks of grain around with me, and buy things with them. If all the members of a monetary community recognise that this money can be used at any time to purchase a specified quantity of grain, the value of money has been defined even if this is 'only' documented in book-keeping figures. In barter trade, clearing or allocation debits and credits works on the same principle as if the US dollar had been used as a measure of value.

Grain money is connected with how one regards and structures the relationship between agriculture and industry. If we base this on the view of agriculture and industry described in Chapter 5, the measure of value can only be an organically cultivated grain that is consumed in the region where it is produced. By using such grain money, the monetary system is anchored within the limited geographical region and sustainable economy of each country, and thus, without state enforcement, facilitates stable exchange rates.

1.12 Money supply and coverage

Money supply is another important factor. As long as money remains a 'thing' such as coins and bank notes, one can never be sure whether the money supply accords with need. In the era of coinage, lasting from ancient until far into modern times, the supply of money fluctuated depending on whether precious metals could be found and made into coins. Successful warlords such as Alexander the Great and the Romans were able to give a strong boost to the economy by procuring treasures of gold and silver through their conquests and turning these into coins. When money was in short supply, by contrast, vendors had to lower their prices to shift their goods. When this led to a rise in the value of money, hoarding was worthwhile, and circulating money decreased still further. For this reason, money supplies had to be continually regulated; and the governments that created this money often found this task too difficult. Throughout history, money supply has brought about a continual flux between economic prosperity and poverty (boom and bust).

How big must the money supply be? In *World Economy*, Rudolf Steiner stated that the only healthy basis for currency was the sum total of useable means of production with which physical work is undertaken, and with whose help the productivity of working people arises.[25] This could easily be confused with what obtains today, where banks base money on ownership of land and means of production, among other things. Steiner was not referring to something that banks must do when they create money but to actually existing circumstances applying to every means of payment that people have ever used, or ever will. I gain the certainty that I can buy something with my money from the economy's productivity. I know that there are people who work and are equipped with facilities that make their work efficient. Both things are needed: people and means of production. These two factors constitute the only real, comprehensive basis of money. This applies specifically also to the service sector that has increased to such an extent since Steiner's day. In economic terms, administration, organisation, education, training and research are bound up with means of production. They perform something through invention of and improvements to the means of production, and through their purposeful use. Today's money is secured by ownership rights to real estate and means of production. In future, the economy's productivity should provide real security by ensuring that only as much money arises as is required in purchase transactions.

No regulation of money supply is needed in the case of 'agreement' or 'associative' money, since it always comes into existence where needed for sale and purchase. The quantity of this money arising in the economy can increase when production increases due to new means of production or additional labour force. Then, in fact, the sum of regular incomes and of companies' regular takings increase, and monetary communities set the range limits of purchase money accounts accordingly. If these limits are enlarged, or if new accounts are added, account holders can spend and earn more money. The sum of all range limits within which purchase money accounts can fluctuate, represents the potential quantity of money. The actual quantity of money arises and disappears by virtue of actual incomes and expenditures. This sounds complex but it is merely unaccustomed, and certainly no more complicated than the money system operating today. In this monetary system the supply of money would be regulated by the economic process in which we all participate. It depends on what we do and how much awareness we have of our actions: what will I buy, how much will I buy? What kinds of production do I wish to be involved in and how much of my income will I save? How much of this will I lend, and how much will I give away?

1.13 Reforms

Monetary reforms affect the very heart of the economy and impact on powerful vested interests. It is senseless to attack our modern monetary system. Until we have enough functioning alternatives, every greater or smaller revolution will be followed by a reversion to the old *status quo,* albeit under the control of different powers. The French Revolution and many other revolutions led to military dictatorships. Real innovation can only be prepared and developed by two things: firstly by gathering experience on a small-scale, and secondly by understanding wider ramifications.[26] State currencies must not be abolished, but they can relinquish their monopoly as 'legal tender', and increasingly limit their scope to the domain where they are needed, as we increasingly create agreement currencies in economic life. Then too, governments can participate in alternative money systems, and accept them as taxation payments.

The state's money monopoly, or that of the central bank, makes sense insofar as only the state may create *state money*. This is a proper goal of efforts to create legal tender.[27] But it should not exclude the possibility of private money systems. This would lead to healthy competition, and people would use the form of money that they consider right. In this regard the theory of free banking (where banks can issue their own paper currency without restriction), the extreme opposite position to the theory of legal state tender, contains a partial truth.[28] In competition between money systems it would become apparent whether people prefer a currency created by private banks to enrich themselves or money systems for the common good.

Today's state monopoly chiefly benefits those involved in speculative trading. They profit from a money system that makes no clear distinction between purchase and loan money, nor separates it administratively. Speculative capital increase only functions, in fact, if one can hoard purchase money, keep it back from circulation and then either lend it to gain interest or use it for speculative stock market and currency exchange trading. But if financial crises continue to be get worse, it is not entirely out of the question that resistance to a relaxation of the money monopoly can be overcome.

If we allow money to arise within the economy, there will be many currencies ranging from local and regional ones through to others used in global trade which already exist as barter organisations. In his book *The Future of Money*, Bernard Lietaer has convincingly demonstrated this. He envisages a future currency model of four levels:

◊ Global currency
◊ Three multinational currencies (euro, yuan, dollar)
◊ National (state) currencies
◊ Complementary regional currencies

These four levels already exist. But the important thing is what weight the four types of currency carry: whether currencies created within the economy increase in importance and whether the State monetary monopoly is relaxed.

These currencies can exist alongside each other, as today national currencies co-exist. Money makes it possible for all to produce for all – that is, for the world at large – and renders the economy a single whole even though there are many different currencies. Between currencies based on the value of grain, it is easier to adhere to fixed exchange rates, thus avoiding the fluctuating exchange rates that today favour speculation and criminal activity. By going down this route it is possible for a global monetary system to emerge – as needed by the world economy – without central governance or predominance of one national currency.[29] In currencies created by monetary communities, we can basically expect there to be a contractually agreed, federalist structure. The content of such contracts cannot be derived from abstract theory but will be a matter for those who actually conclude them. The whole organisation of economic life can be founded on this principle.

Money is an important factor in economic life, but not its source and origin. Just by tinkering with the monetary system it would never be possible to remedy the whole economy. Economic life involves production, market and consumption. The following chapters are therefore necessary not just as a supplement to what has been said so far but as a basis for understanding monetary processes.

2. Labour and Income

2.1 Practical experiences

In this section we will look at practical experiences in Steiner-Waldorf Schools in Switzerland, seeing how these can easily be applied to other enterprises including commercial ones. These schools have taken decisive steps towards overcoming the wage system. The incomes of teachers and employees are not regarded as staffing costs but as distributive allocation of the enterprise's income. Prior to the start of the school year, needs are assessed; and this assessment is governed by general and detailed rules that have been agreed by all participants. The income of teachers and other staff depends on the size of their families and the number of their children. Other family incomes are subtracted. Consideration must be given to retirement pensions. Rather than being based on minimum needs, as calculated for debt enforcement or social benefits, the income agreed aims to allow a modest but good way of life. The needs of all participants are totalled, and this overall figure is included in the school's annual budget – which shows whether the expected income will cover what is required. If not, savings and restrictions have to be considered. This whole way of working has proved successful for many years, but is so unusual that it is necessary to examine below what underlies it, and what it signifies for the broader social context.

2.2 Separating labour and income

In lectures in 1905, and in an essay published in 1906, Rudolf Steiner spoke of the Fundamental Social Law and said that it requires 'a complete separation between working for one's fellow human beings and having a certain level of income.'[1] There are very different views about how this requirement might be realised in practice. Some seek to base it on the idea of the threefold social order, separating work and income by administering one of these (though which?) in the economic realm and the other in the rights sphere. This already happens to some extent when the state gives an income to those unable to work, funding this from taxation.

Opposed to this is another view: that the separation between labour and income is something that must be undertaken within the economy and gradually realised as the Fundamental Social Law envisages. Here only generally valid laws should be involved in the same way as in all economic processes. The justification for this view is complex, as we will see. Let us first remind ourselves of the precise words of this Fundamental Social Law:

> The well-being of a community working together will be greater, the less the individual claims the proceeds of his work for himself, that is, the more of these proceeds he hands over to his fellow-workers, and the more his own needs are satisfied, not by his own work but by the work done by others.

This is not a law equivalent in any way to state legislation or an ethical requirement but should be seen as a kind of natural law. It does not stipulate how something *should* be but describes how it *is*. Nevertheless we can deduce a postulation from it. The words 'The more ... the more ...' tell us that this is something that can increasingly be realised, though not by a blanket political enactment:

Wherever this law manifests, wherever someone works in accordance with it to the extent possible in the position he occupies within the human community, good will follow, even if only to a small degree in an individual instance. And only from isolated effects arising in this way will wholesome progress come about throughout society.

2.3 An 'earnings' or a 'needs' economy?

To examine this further we must start from very basic considerations. I enter a store and am astonished at the wealth of available products. Everything is so temptingly presented that a desire rises up in me to possess what I see. But actually I don't want these things at all – they would hold me back from what I really want. A suspicion occurs to me that a great deal of purchases are simply triggered by suggestive advertising rather than because the things themselves are needed. If I look around a bit more in the modern world I might notice the heavy traffic on a motorway at the weekend. How much of it is really necessary – even if for leisure or entertainment – and how much just idle time-filling? Even if it's pointless, everything I consume has to be produced, and invariably there is a price to pay in terms of the environment and human labour.

This type of consumption as leisure activity has many causes, but one of the most important is that the modern economy is fundamentally oriented to earnings rather than need. This is a fundamental distinction. The doctrine of the earnings economy asserts that all people seek gain, and only work because they get a wage in return. It states that one thing is only produced because something else cannot be sold. Rudolf Steiner recommends turning economic thinking on its head and transforming the earnings economy into a needs economy. This change is so fundamental that we would have to see many economic processes in a quite different way. Need as orientation and impulse for the economy arises from human culture and is a given in the economy. It must not be induced or created by the economy. This means that all commercial companies (not just charitable institutions) require an ideal objective: their primary goal must be to meet a real need. No one should have to do work that does not help meet a need. The creation of jobs through economic growth – which many strive for as a political aim – makes no economic sense and is socially inept, since it would be better if the work undertaken were transferred to the social and cultural sphere where it is urgently needed.

This book tries to show that many aspects of, and factors in economic thinking must change if we are to see the economy consistently in terms of need.

2.4 Production factors and products

Labour, land and capital are termed 'production factors' in economic theory, and rightly so insofar as labour, land with all its natural opportunities, and capital, are the prerequisites for economic production, but are not products in themselves. Without land (nature), labour and capital, no goods or services can be produced. However, in themselves they are not finished products. Only when we apply our labour in a particular location to earthly things, often also using labour-supporting means (capital), are useable goods and services created that 'come onto the market' and, if there is a need for them, can be sold.

Land, labour and capital are valuable, but in a way quite different from goods. We are not at all accustomed to making this clear distinction between production factors and finished products. Land, labour and capital only become economically valuable when we involve them in productive activity. Labour alone, even if we exert ourselves to the greatest degree – as in sport – is economically unproductive. It becomes valuable if it transforms earthly materials in a productive way. Nature too (the land with all its possible uses and hidden resources) has no economic value by itself, acquiring this only when we change it through labour in a way that we can use and consume (see Section 3.6 on ground rent on how this value is determined). The way economic values arise and disappear must be observed in the same way that one observes flowing forms and currents in a streaming body of water.[2]

In the economy based on division of labour, goods and services are exchanged so that they can be used by anyone who needs them. As a means of exchange, money facilitates complex and intricate trading relationships. In exchange it is always a matter of comparing values. Money facilitates this comparison in exact figures. It allows economic values to be measured by giving them a price. The market is the place where prices arise through comparisons of value.

Production factors $\longrightarrow$ Production $\longrightarrow$ Market		
Land (nature)		
Labour	$\longrightarrow$ Values of goods $\longrightarrow$ Price relationships	
Capital		

A kilogramme of wheat is valuable in the first instance because people can eat it. Whenever things are produced, they acquire a value as useable goods. It is important to get a clear grasp of this concept of value, and not to confuse it with the price of a commodity. This is not easy for us since we prefer to recognise only what we can measure and count. The nutritional value of a kilo of wheat is something concrete. If we then say that wheat costs X, we now have an abstract value concept. The same X can stand for the most diverse range of other products, and remains the same for all of them. Market prices do not express the real usefulness of particular goods but only the value relationships between them. For instance, prices tell us that a pair of shoes is equal in value to a hundred litres of milk, etc. Every price expresses the relationship it has with all other prices. And so we can say that economic values result from production processes. We can describe them and qualitatively evaluate them by placing them into their economic context. Price, by contrast, is abstracted from these concrete economic values, and renders them comparable. It only gives us a quantitative evaluation of goods and services.

Land and labour cannot be manufactured as goods can. If we nevertheless assign a price to them, as we do nowadays, and exchange them for money in markets (the land and labour markets), we are exchanging production factors for finished products, making land, labour and capital into purchasable commodities. But here we must distinguish three categories of production factors:
   1. values of production factors,
   2. values of products, and
   3. prices of commodities.

We can only calculate prices in figures. The other two values must be seen instead as functions that we can describe but not calculate.

Although prices are determined by market processes, and an individual cannot 'set' them, we can evaluate or assess them. We can say if they are too high or low, or just right, and have a precise measure for this. Prices reach their correct level, in fact, if the manufacturers and vendors of a commodity or service can live from it until they are able to produce and sell another such good or service. Here we are not thinking of a minimum standard of living, an 'existential minimum' but of a standard of living matching the general level of our culture. Rudolf Steiner assigned this evaluation an important place in economic theory when he referred to it as a 'basic economic unit' or 'primal cell' of the economy.[3] Where land is concerned, this formulation cannot be applied since land is not produced. When we buy or lease land, we do not acquire a commodity, but only a right of use. The proprietor of the land has the right to exclude all others from use of this land. In this context, Rudolf Steiner never tired of pointing out that rights cannot be exchange for goods, and therefore cannot be purchased.

2.5 Limits of the market economy

The term market is used to describe the core area of economics where goods and services are exchanged. Technology enables human labour to be divided in complex ways and rendered effective. This is only possible because the products of labour can be exchanged in equally complex ways, so that we do not have to make everything we need for ourselves. The validity of a market economy must be restricted to this core area of the economy. In one direction the market borders on the production realm, where production factors are used in a way that enables productivity to arise. In the other direction, we meet the field of income distribution and consumption.

> In pure economic activity we are only concerned with production, consumption and the circulation between these two. But this means nothing other than that the intrinsic life of the economy is concerned only with the circulation of produced goods which, as they circulate, become commodities. We are concerned here with the

2. LABOUR AND INCOME

circulation of commodities. A product, the need
for which affects its price, acquires a certain value
within the social organism, and is ... commodity.[4]

Production	Market	Yield
Goods and services are produced through: 1. Use of land (nature) 2. Labour 3. Capital which makes labour productive	Commodities and services are priced through exchange	Distribution/ allocation of profit (after deduction of company reserves): 1. Private income 2. Social welfare 3. Donations to cultural domain
Area of performance	Area of sale/ purchase	Area of consumption

The market economy within the overall economy

In the middle column, where goods and services of equal
value are exchanged with each other, there is reciprocity.
This is a fundamental principle of economic activity. Rudolf
Steiner pointed out that in every exchange or sale (unless
unhealthy power factors are at work) both partners gain
advantage or benefit. I buy merchandise because I can do
more with it than with the money I have to pay for it. For
sellers the opposite is true: they wish to get rid of their
merchandise and are in need of money.[5] This is the goal of
every sale discussion: the negotiating partners both wish to
make a bargain.

Prior to the market and thereafter, we are concerned with
one-sided processes. Nowadays we artificially bring labour
and wages into direct connection in the market economy,
doing so because we think that people are unwilling to work
if they are not paid for it. In fact, when we actually undertake
labour, this is not the case at all. The bus driver stops at the

bus stop so that people can get in and out; a factory worker connects up a cable so that appliances can function, etc. We wish to accomplish our work because humanity needs it. If we suspect or even perceive that this is not so, our work becomes an inner burden to us. This real economic value of our work cannot be encompassed simply in figures. Figures, that is prices, only come into play when we find purchasers for our products to whom we can sell them. The price is not just determined by the production but also by the degree to which others want the product. This only becomes apparent in the market, where the values of diverse merchandise are measured against each other with using a unit of money applicable to all the commodities. If I hear or read that a watch costs a thousand pounds or dollars, this is not an isolated consideration, since I see the price of the watch in connection with my financial situation or with that of others, and these situations originate in other realms of the economy than does the watch. The market and the prices make the economy into a whole system.

In mainstream economics, the production earning is divided between the three production factors. Economists speak of labour income share, return on capital and ground rent (see Section 3.6). However, calculating back from the earnings to these factors is only possible theoretically, and does not correspond to the actual processes involved. Private income cannot be regarded as the price of labour since it does not belong to the production of goods and services but to their consumption. It stands at the other end of the economy and must arise from a contractually regulated distribution of company earnings. Thus we can see, in this approach, that labour and income are separate insofar as both are one-directional acts with the character of performance without a reciprocal performance. In the economy there are indeed services or performance without a service in return, and these are of great significance.

The values of labour, land and capital that cannot be measured in terms of reciprocal performance can be called productivity values, so as to distinguish them from the values of goods. These productivity values cannot be calculated in money sums, but must initially be described as follows: The land is suitable for producing X tonnes of rye or wheat per hectare; and, depending on location, X working hours will be required for this. In this way we obtain a tangible, clear concept of value that must become as fully comprehensible to us as monetary figures.

2.6 Labour law

The concept of labour can cause much confusion if we do not carefully distinguish between the legal and economic meanings of the word. Labour law is not concerned with the product or outcome of work but with the working person, and here we can speak of 'labour force' rather than 'output'. If I take a job and sign an employment contract, I declare my willingness to undertake the work my employer gives me in accordance with the job description and appointment profile. I make my work available to the employer, and this employment relationship is primarily governed by the dependency of the employee on the employer. The employee's rights are however protected by numerous legislative conditions (for instance about working hours, maternity leave, age, notice period, health and safety, insurance, etc.). The laws impose duties on both employers and employees.

The extract below from a lecture Steiner gave to workers at the Daimler plant in Stuttgart on April 25, 1919 shows clearly how he distinguished between labour law and output:

> If, instead of economic life dictating labour,
> economic life is determined by decisions workers

themselves make within a democratic state in regard to their labour, then an important requirement has been met. People will object that economic life then becomes dependent on labour laws and rights. That's true, but this will be a healthy dependency, just as natural a one as our dependency on the natural world. Before workers enter the factory, they will know how much and how long they will need to work, and will no longer have any need at all to negotiate with an employer about the amount and kind of work to be done. They will only need to discuss distribution of what is produced in collaboration with the employer. This could form a labour contract. Contracts will only govern distribution of what has been produced, not labour itself.[6]

The capacity to work is a human attribute, a part of our intrinsic nature. If people find that others are dictating their labour and can compel them to do something they do not wish to – for instance, produce weapons or poisons – then they feel that their rights are being infringed. These rights must not be rendered inactive through the wielding of economic power. Power over others must be comprehensively replaced by laws and rights. Current laws need enlarging. Working hours as laid down in law are far too long today – half would be sufficient to produce and perform what is actually needed.[7] The right to reject an offer of work is also legitimate where good grounds can be given.

At the same time a right to work exists. We feel this right to be violated if we are dismissed from a job and left unemployed. An employer ought not to lay off employees without trying to find them another job. An individual employer is not in a position to do this alone and should therefore enter into association with others in order to participate contractually in an organisation involved in the overall economy.

On the other hand, an obligation exists to accomplish work. We consider it unjust when some receive support from society but contribute nothing to it, despite being in a position to do so. The right and the duty to work are not enshrined in legislation, nor is this necessary. But if we reflect on our feeling of justice we will act accordingly in our economic conduct. In concrete terms this means that freeloaders should not be compelled to work but should do this voluntarily; and that they would be willing to do so if they had learned to consider their own feelings of justice rather than subscribing to the 'normal' view that one only does what one is compelled to do by law.

Not only rights, but duties too, are generally recognised to be part of the rights sphere. If we promise something, we ought to fulfil it. We are free to promise what we wish to. We can voluntarily take on obligations, but they are no less obligations for that. Such conditions, known to us in civil law, are a model. But there are also rights and duties in which we are all equal and that we become aware of when we acknowledge others to be human beings like ourselves. Every right is the basis for duties. If we accord a right to someone, we undertake a duty to respect this right. Regarding the relationship between rights and duties, Rudolf Steiner made the following innovative and far-reaching statement:

> We live however in an era when people prefer
> to speak of their rights than of their duties ...
> Duty is the opposite idea from right. A time will
> follow ours when, due to the influence of the
> anthroposophical spritual worldview, duties and
> obligations will come into their own. And only
> in the future, albeit one still a long way off, will
> movements come to exist that emphasise duties far
> more than rights.[8]

Rudolf Steiner regarded the freely accepted duty to work as self-evident. But this only comes properly into play if we develop a sense of rights and duties in our specific interpersonal relations in society.

> No legislated or enforced rights will ever develop
> our sense of duty. Only the sense of justice
> arising between equals, between one mature
> and responsible person and the other, in living
> interaction, will give people the keen will to work.
> And this sense of justice will need to incorporate
> labour into itself.

The duty to work is therefore a matter of our sense of justice.

> And a sense of our freely elected duty to work is
> the only thing that can bring about a renewal in our
> lives, as opposed to this duty being imposed upon
> us, which will simply throttle every sense of justice
> in us.[9]

This sense arises when we learn to see and understand what humanity needs. Steiner was opposed to imposing a duty to work by legislation. Laws, he believed, should only enshrine what lives in everyone's inherent sense of justice if they do not suppress it. If we regard justice as being only what legislation dictates – the norms determined by the state's legislative power – this sense of justice cannot develop. On one occasion Rudolf Steiner told the Christian Community priests to be:

> In my book, *The Philosophy of Freedom*, the life of
> rights, too, is founded on the individual human
> being who works entirely out of his own inner
> dictates. One of the first, and in fact one of the
> most brilliant critics of this book ... wrote simply
> that my whole view would lead to a theoretical

anarchism. Naturally modern people will believe this to be so. Why? Because they lack all real, God-imbued social trust; because they cannot grasp something that is most vital of all nowadays, which is this: if we can really bring people to speak out of their inmost being, then harmony will arise amongst human beings not through their own will but through the divine ordering of the world. Disharmony arises because people actually do not speak from their inmost depths ...[10]

2.7 Overcoming the labour market

When Steiner energetically proposes abolishing wage dependency that forces us into work, this is not just about legal protection of working people but also about *economic performance*. Strict mutuality holds sway in the market economy in that services are exchanged with reciprocal services. This market economy connection should not obtain between the performance of the individual and his income. The two are only of equal dimensions in overall statistics, that is, as social income and national product.

Wage as a connection between work and income is something artificial that we have become fully accustomed to. Wage is considered as remuneration for work, we could say its 'purchase price'. We speak of the labour market, and find this term in every newspaper. As in every market, an accommodation occurs between supply and demand, which is meant to give rise to the price level, or in this case the wage. These structures and procedures however prevent us from learning to think and feel socially. We are integrated into the 'labour market' like a cog in a machine. This mechanistic paradigm will continue to apply as long we are limited to a purely egotistic outlook, for as egotists human beings can be included in calculations; and prevailing economic theory today (as we can read in every textbook) relies on this distorted view of the human being. And yet we are also capable of parental love, and willingness to help others is a 'normal' human capacity. It is known that unpaid work is roughly equal to the sum of all remunerated work. In Switzerland, for example, unpaid work in the home alone accounts for around 40 per cent of the national economy's value creation.[11]

In remunerated work, too, egotism is far from being the only motive. Every work requires a high degree of selflessness in the form of interest, concentration, attention, care, precision, perseverance and a willingness to do things that are difficult or uncomfortable, etc. Many people, perhaps even most, do not choose their profession for wage-related reasons but because they enjoy the work and find meaning and purpose in it.

Nowadays there are minimum wages for lower-paid workers, and labour agreements that ease the pressure of market rules. But it is interesting that the 'labour market' is used as a justification for the top wages, many of which are not related to productivity. A manager who earns several million dollars or pounds a year has a great deal of responsibility and to a large degree determines the success of an enterprise, but he does not work correspondingly more than an employee earning $50,000. So why should the manager get several million? Because – it is said – he would be cherry-picked by competitors, perhaps going to another country to be paid a higher wage. Managers' wages are said to be the 'going market rate'; but in fact these ludicrously high wages ought to show us how unusable and estranged from life the concept of the labour market is.

In ordinary life we are quite aware that the idea of the productivity-related wage gets us nowhere. In the social welfare state we give an income to those who cannot work;

and repeatedly a desire surfaces to separate work and income. Louis Blanc, though not the first to do so, gave expression to this desire in his book, *Organization of Labour*. The phrase 'Each according to his capacities, to each according to his needs!' became the goal of socialism, also as expressed by Karl Marx who described it in 1875 in his *Critique of the Gotha Programme* as the ultimate aim of Communism. This idea is an example of an intellectually conceived Utopian wish. Rudolf Steiner always rejected Utopian thinking, and took a quite different approach to the separation between work and income. This is why, when describing the Fundamental Social Law, he did not speak of a social or even moral ideal but of a law that applies in a way similar to a law of nature, and must be gleaned from actual conditions and realities.

The Communists tried to achieve their Utopian aims by enforcing state control of the economy. Market economics, on the other hand, holds the view that human egotism should be given free rein in the economy since this alone will give rise to productivity. However, the social tasks that egotism cannot deal with are still assigned to the state in the 'social market economy'. It is worth noting that both concepts seek to separate income from work either entirely or to some degree, and instead draw on the state's support. But is the state the only right means of doing this?

Work and income belong to the economy and there appear as opposite poles, with work belonging to production and income to consumption. Work flows into the economy and income derives from it. If we wish to separate them, this must happen within the economic process. This is the task that we have to solve in our time taking full account of the nature of both aspects, ensuring that the outcome is both economically and socially beneficial. Social concerns for the common welfare belong to the economy itself! Instead of delegating this care to the state, we must learn, as economically productive people, to take on this social task ourselves. This may require a long process of change, but leads towards a humane future.

2.8 Changes in accounting

Accounts help us to become aware of economic processes insofar as these can be measured in figures. It is extremely helpful for our social cohesion to be able to objectively record our economic relationships in numerical terms. If we are in conflict with one another, we keep our accounts as secret as possible, and in many human relationships today this is the case. But if those who are connected economically have the opportunity to examine each other's accounts, they have a basis for social collaboration.[12] Accounting can render economic processes transparent, and this is its sole task despite the fact that it is often misused to conceal the truth. The tax authorities have always known this, and therefore ask companies to submit their end-of-year accounts according to legally stipulated rules. Transparent accounting is the first step required for the kind of financial collaboration which the present and future require of us.

Nowadays the normal thing is for wages (also of managers) to be recorded as staffing costs. This means that the incomes people live from appear as cost factor within the company. But in reality, human existence is the *goal* of the economy. The aim of the economy, after all, is to meet human needs – that is the generally accepted definition of economics. In business economics, by contrast, the company's goal is regarded as *profit*. These two concepts, need and profit, contradict each other in modern economic thinking since, in relation to the production factors of land, labour and capital, one speaks of 'factor costs'. In relation to labour, let us examine this more carefully.

Starting from a sole trader we see that, as owner of his

business it is quite obvious that he lives from the profit or net income which he achieves through his work. In his case, work and income are directly related. He does not record his takings as staffing costs, nor does he regard himself as a 'cost factor' for his business. His profit and loss account has the following structure:

Expenditure:
  Overheads
 	
Profit:
  Own use
  Reserves
  Capital increase
	Income:
	Sale of goods and services

Sole trader profit and loss account

In a company with employees, wages (including salaries of directors) are usually recorded as staffing costs, while profit belongs to the owners of the company – the shareholders in a company with share capital (corporation).

Expenditure:
  Overheads
  Wages and salaries
 	
Profit
	Income:
	Sale of goods and services

Normal profit and loss account for a company with numerous employees

If people in large companies with many employees are not to be calculated as cost factors, this means that wages and salaries need to be transferred from expenditure to profit. But this is different from the case of the sole trader, since the service provided by the company arises from the collaboration of all the employees. The division of labour through which the modern economy becomes ever more productive cannot be imagined without collaboration. One person, whether manager, constructor or manual worker, will achieve nothing alone. Therefore labour and income are no longer directly linked in a single worker. To reflect this collaboration, the division between work and income also needs to be expressed in the accounts.

Expenditure: Overheads Cost of materials Energy Administration Rent-interest Depreciation Reserves Repayment of loans Sundries *Profit:* Share for staff Donations to cultural life Donations to social welfare	*Income:* Sale of goods and services

New way of presenting the profit and loss account for a company with numerous employees

This change in recording of the accounts is a first practical measure that can be introduced in every company if people wish to do so. Naturally the auditor and tax authorities will shake their heads, and will demand that the accounts must be presented to them in the same way as previously. But within the company management itself, and among all employees, accounts can be recorded in this new way, so that those involved are aware of this new reality and give expression to it. This would go a long way towards creating a new way of thinking. Instead of asking what the cost of labour is, one would learn to ask, can enough income arise some work to ensure that all who contribute to it can live from it? Labour will then change from being a cost to a condition of the income. Only this income and not labour, can be measured in terms of money.

2.9 Profit distribution

Financial abuses have given the concept of profit a nasty aftertaste. But in fact profit is simply the excess income over expenditure, that is simply the result of production. This no longer belongs to the production side but indicates how much can be consumed. To distribute profit means to lead it over into consumption. Here I want to describe how profit can be distributed if the income of all staff is contained in it. I will offer possible scenarios, not fixed schemas, for what counts in each case is what the people concerned want. Only some perspectives and aids to help judgment can be offered here, to help people form clearer ideas about what they actually want.

Nowadays, profit distribution is a matter for the proprietors, for instance the shareholders of a company. Their goal is not usually consumption but the accumulation of capital. The allocation of dividends to external 'owners' of the company is something that should be relinquished as a matter of principle. Companies in which the shareholders determine the use of profit are a bad basis for creating new forms such as those described here. Since it is common today amongst shareholders to appropriate financial power through majority shareholdings, the greatest resistance to views proposed here can be expected from this quarter.

Determining the level of private consumption

The net income or profit contains more than the private income of co-workers. The first step therefore involves making the following clear distinctions between the uses of profit:

a) Private incomes
b) Donations to cultural institutions
c) Social payments for people who receive too little support from statutory benefits, e.g. additional incomes for single mothers
d) Reserves for improving the company
e) Repayment of debts

This profit distribution is a matter for all the workers who have together created the company yield, and all of them have a right to decide. If the meeting has been well prepared, its decision can even be formulated in terms where an overwhelming majority is in favour while all others declare themselves willing to support it. Then there will only be assenting votes and abstentions. Those who abstain express by this means that, although they would have preferred a different outcome, they can nevertheless live with this decision. In contrast to unanimity we might call this form of decision-making 'consensual'. It often occurs in daily life, even where it seems that a majority decision has been taken. As opposed to the procedure in a 'crucial vote', consensus dispenses with compulsion and requires tact and consideration between people, which in turn creates trust. Real consensus is not possible in a climate of dispute and annoyance, but where it proves possible such an approach is a wonderful chance for each person to think not only of himself, but also of others.

2. LABOUR AND INCOME

General rules for the apportioning
of private consumption

In relation to every social measure we adopt we need to distinguish between drawing up rules and applying these rules in individual instances. In the case of profit distribution, a difficult area to agree on, rules are especially helpful. If such rules apply to all equally, then every person involved has the right to have their say; and so here too the consensual decision-making method can be used. Every community can establish its own rules. Below I offer examples to help readers picture some of the ways in which this might work. This also makes it easier to look for different solutions. These are merely *possible* approaches.

The needs of every colleague or worker and their family must be met. I'm not thinking here of some minimum wage or basic income, but of an income that makes sufficient money available to all so that, for instance, they can also pay for education or make donations to causes they support. A just income for all ought to be high enough to enable each person to finance education, research and social activities as individually chosen. Currently the government deprives us of full responsibility through taxation which is then distributed by bureaucrats according to general laws.

Incomes do not have to be equal, but just. There should be clearly perceived reasons for differences of income, for instance, professional experience, or levels of responsibility which company managers or directors have. If they make mistakes, this can greatly damage the company. They are entrusted with the company's capital, and, if they have taken out loans as personal credit, they run a personal risk. They are not just employed managers but entrepreneurs (see Section 4.3). Like independent artists and intellectuals, an important factor for them is whether they meet with understanding and recognition for their innovations and ideas. Without intelligent company management, a great deal of work accomplished in a company would be a waste of time and go nowhere. While it is true in general that everyone makes free, voluntary use of their skills, profit allocation can take account of diverse levels of skill and experience, years of service, further training, degrees of responsibility and personal risk. One must welcome competent colleagues. The rules allow scope for individual decisions. But we are always concerned here with distribution of the overall yield, and not with payment for an individual's performance.

A maximum income can be set, for instance, at a certain sum above the basic need per person, so that income differentials do not become excessive. If a further surplus is to be distributed, this can be done proportionately to the income already distributed, or to the basic agreed income. In the case of part-time work, due account can be taken of the working hours of each colleague. If someone only works part-time by choice, they only have a claim to 50 per cent of their and their family's needs.

These general rules, contractually agreed, give each worker and their family a legal entitlement. When such rules are being drawn up it is important to recognise that differences exist, and that not everyone will 'earn' the same. Workers can use these rules to determine, for instance, that managers and experienced colleagues will receive more than others, in line with conditions agreed by consensus.

Applying these rules in individual cases

It is usually not possible for everyone together to judge an individual situation, so a different procedure is needed for this. It is conceivable to form a group of trusted colleagues, composed of people knowledgeable in their field who therefore have the confidence of all workers. They may be long-serving staff, or they may have some insight into company management. These trusted people can negotiate the individual income with each staff member. They form a picture of the specific situation, but apply the same rules in every case. This equality of treatment is an important element for the trust that this group enjoys. Rules always have to be interpreted, similar to the way in which judges interpret and apply laws. In fact, this work of the trusted group resembles that of judges. Rudolf Steiner assigned judges not to the democratic state but to cultural life, and this principle must apply here too.[13] In small companies, where all staff know each other well, it may be that everyone's income is available and freely perused by all. In large companies this would not work since not everyone can gain sufficient insight into each individual situation. In this case the work of the trusted group will remain confidential. External checks and balances can be established. Hybrid forms are also conceivable and have proven their worth, for instance, where the trusted colleagues first assess individual cases and then submit the outcome to all.

Where incomes have previously been at a fairly reasonable level, large downward adjustments should not be introduced. Where this is necessary, it can be done gradually so that people have time to change their lifestyle accordingly. The aim of every company must be to ensure that all staff can live well. If this is not the case, internal or industry-wide measures must be taken, as described in Section 2.10. The desired minimum profit level must be formulated in each year's budget so that staff know what their likely income is to be, and so that private drawings during the year can be paid as regularly as wages.

General, democratically decided rules, and their non-democratic application by a trusted group have proven their worth in some Steiner-Waldorf Schools both in relation to parental contributions and teacher incomes. Experience has shown, above all, the importance of elaborating rules and organisational structures with the greatest care. If carefully organised, such structures function well in these schools even where funds are tight, and both parents and teachers are willing to make sacrifices. In Western Europe, though, enough money is available to provide sufficient incomes for all. It is only a matter of whether we want this. Redistribution of current incomes is not the primary concern, although this is of importance in many cases. More significant are the new procedures through which we can learn to recognise and assert not only our own interests but also those of others. In the long term this will lead us out of our social plight.

This approach used to be quite normal for some professions. In any village it was quite clear to all that the minister and teacher needed enough to live on, and they were supported by voluntary gifts because people wanted this. Today we have sunk so deeply into egotism that we have to make untiring efforts to develop a new way of thinking. This new thinking ought to be cultivated through training and education within companies, for otherwise people will refuse to join in such schemes. The transition from 'wage entitlement' to needs-based income will not come about without objections and reversals, but this is no reason to give up the attempt.

One counter-argument is likely to be this: 'If income is separated from work, people will lose interest in their work.' Here too education is required so that people see the purpose and meaning of their work: that it is useful and meets a need, albeit not their own. The reality of the economy based on a division of labour is that we always work for others, not ourselves.

The separation between work and income means that all people can acquire a good deal of independence that is denied them today by their wage dependency. This can be achieved when all colleagues or workers live from a company's profit in the same way as is usual for freelancers or sole traders.

Living from this profit means having an independent income. By contrast, labour itself quite rightly relies on lack of independence. Here the work itself is the focus, and each person's position accords here with his skills or abilities. One person will be more independent, and manage the work, while another is less so and performs the work. There are intermediate levels and hybrid situations between managing and performing the work. It is right for all to have an equal say in establishing rules that govern income distribution. In company management, by contrast, equality of decision-making is out place, for there it is each person's capacities and professional competence which matters.

In modern employment contracts, work and income are coupled together. In future they must be clearly separated, possibly in two different contracts. Two committees can be formed here for the company as party to the contract. The company management concludes a contract relating to the job and the work to be performed. It selects a new staff member for their skills to fill the needs of the company. The group of trusted colleagues checks the income required for the new worker and draws up a contract with the latter stating what share of profit will be paid. Thus each co-worker is connected to the company in two clearly distinguished ways.

2.10 Industry-wide measures through associations

'Just' income distribution could only be introduced with a single measure at one go, if the state enforced this by a universal intervention. But if we wish to develop human community on the basis of autonomy and freedom, we can approach the task gradually and from various directions. One of several measures needed in terms of the Fundamental Social Law has been described here as profit distribution in each company. Further provisions would require intercompany collaboration so as to work towards the creation of healthy prices in the market place.

The target prices of goods and services have the greatest impact on people's incomes. These are determined in the market and cannot be set unilaterally through price calculations by the selling company. However, once these prices have arisen, they can be evaluated if one has a measure of value. One can only affect what *underlies* pricing, in particular the scope of production and thus the range on offer. The prices themselves do not have to be directly fixed but only observed in terms of the 'basic economic unit' or 'primal cell'. As mentioned in Section 2.4, Rudolf Steiner described the 'true price' in relation to this primal cell in the following way:

> I once tried to formulate what a right price would
> look like. Of course I don't mean that it should be
> determined in an abstract way. As I have suggested,
> it will be determined by the realities of life. But I
> said this: the right price for a particular product
> within society, thus for a particular commodity,
> is one which enables the producer to ensure the
> livelihood of self and family, and to meet all
> their needs until the same person has once again
> produced the same product.[14]

This formulation shows that the time we need to produce something is of primary importance. It is of course right to think of a person's hours of work as a part of their life. But nature and capital also play a part in production besides work. Without capital and intelligent inventions, goods would remain expensive – too expensive. So prices must make it possible to sufficiently sustain cultural or spiritual life, the source of inventiveness. Nature too must be taken into due account through care, environmentally friendly usage and recycling of waste. In this way we can enlarge Steiner's price formula by adding the needs of spiritual or cultural life and of nature. This accords fully with his outlook, and emphasises the importance of healthy prices for the net income of the economy, and thus for income distribution.

In agriculture today we have an example of unhealthy prices, and state subsidies will, in the long run, not provide a helpful alternative to a healthy price ratio. What, with Rudolf Steiner, we call a 'basic economic unit' or 'primal cell' of the economy is no longer such a distant prospect today, since we now have fair trading, which is promoted precisely for this reason – because we know that prices have a vital impact on the incomes of working and their families. The word 'fair' here expresses the fact that when we buy and sell we wish to pay heed to others' interests as well as our own.

Rudolf Steiner does not use the expression 'fair price' but speaks instead of a just, true or also objective price, which cannot be fixed as such nor determined theoretically:

> In the economic domain what counts especially is that solutions are not found by fixing or determining things in some way – let us say by a study of statistics and suchlike – but that they are drawn directly from life itself. Let me give an example. Everyone knows that an article, a commodity, becomes too cheap in economic circulation if too many people are producing the same thing, when too much of the same thing is produced; and likewise we all know that goods become too expensive if too few people produce them. This gives us a guideline for finding that objective middle range I spoke about. This happy medium, this objective value cannot be fixed as such. But if associations are created with the aim of gaining practical knowledge of economic life, of studying what is actually happening at any moment, their main task will be to observe how prices rise

or fall. By attending carefully to this rise and fall of prices, associations will be able to negotiate to ensure that a sufficient number of people are involved in a certain branch of production. Through negotiations it will be possible to get enough people working in a branch of production. This cannot be fixed theoretically but can only be determined by ensuring people are involved in the right work. It is human experience itself, therefore, that determines these things. And for this reason one cannot say, either, that this or that is the 'objective' value.

If associations work in this way within economic life, making it one of their obligations to gradually diminish companies that are making prices too cheap, and instead to establish others which produce other commodities, then enough people will be involved in different branches of production. This can only arise through a truly associative life. And then the price for any particular commodity will come closer to an objective level. We can never say that the 'objective' price must be set at this or that level due to this or that condition. All we can say is that when the right human association arises, its work will gradually allow the true price to emerge within the real life of the social organism.[15]

Nowadays we make it a task of the state to redress economic imbalances in society in line with the following idea: in the economy each person strives for profit; and where there are losses and social deficits, the state takes care of them. The task of price monitoring is also considered to be one for the government. In reality it is an especially important task of the economy itself, one that a single company cannot meet on its own but certainly can address in an organisation for intercompany collaboration where companies in diverse areas of the economy network with each other. In the quote above, Steiner gives a detailed account of the associative collaboration between companies as consisting in observing reciprocal price relationships and checking and then discussing what measures can be used to correct unhealthy price relationships.

Prices always express value relationships, for instance between food, clothes, bicycles, clocks, nursing and care services, administrative and consultative work, etc., which are measured in monetary terms. For this reason price monitoring involves a collaboration between diverse areas of the economy. Those who work in one sector are purchasers and consumers of the products of another. This is why, when Rudolf Steiner was proposing a threefold social order after the First World War, he placed importance on diverse sectors, especially agriculture and industry, being represented in the 'associations'. By this means contact is created between production, trade and consumer interests. In relation to price monitoring and the measures arising from it, the interests of individual consumers can most effectively be implemented by company representatives. The industry representative will have an interest in ensuring that agricultural produce is not too expensive for his staff; but at the same time he wants agriculture to be in a position to buy the products of his industry.

Supply and demand are real elements in the market and determine prices. In market economy theory it is said that the reverse is true as well: that prices also affect and regulate supply and demand. In theory this looks very neat. But if we listen to the daily financial news we see that this kind of regulation is associated with economic and social misfortune, bankruptcies, company closures and unemployment. Large-scale productive forces are lost in consequence. The market is not a reliable authority, which we can trust in blindly, for adjusting production to need. People engaged in economic activity are the real authority. Associations have the task of adjusting production to need in such a way as to create prices that are as close as possible to the 'true' prices. If a particular form of production is to be reduced or increased, workers must be moved from one sector to another. Job placement is not the task of government departments. If people have to be laid off in one company, it is the task of intercompany collaboration to offer them places where they are needed; and this applies also to cultural and social professions.

One individual's rationale is not enough for judging prices since it is never a matter of a price in isolation but always of a whole complex of price relationships. In the economy, individual interests are a necessity. It is the task of associations to balance these. Egotism cannot be excluded from the economy but simply needs to be balanced. What one person needs is something only they can know; but the others must try to understand these needs. All people, insofar as they are engaged in production or consumption, participate in the associative organisation, as we saw clearly, already, in Chapter 1 on money management.

Associations do not dictate the economy from above but make contractual regulations between equal parties. A family fund distributing child allowances could easily also be an institution of intercompany collaboration. A further area for intercompany collaboration involves balancing advantages and disadvantages of particular locations. In many sectors of the economy, this plays a major role, particularly so in agriculture. One cannot suggest to hill farmers that they should go somewhere better. If, for instance, farms sited in valleys and mountains, those on more fertile loam and less fertile sand, have a collaborative organisation together, they could set up a location compensation fund whose task would be to balance the resulting differences in income.

It is interesting that state subsidies for agriculture also

aim to correct income levels. And yet if, as is the case today, the level of agricultural prices is generally too low, even in businesses in fertile regions favoured with good climates, then income subsidies are the wrong route to go down. They falsify the whole economy by merely covering up and thus reinforcing the basic problem: the price disparity between industry and agriculture. This is caused by fundamental errors in the economy and political order, which must be addressed and remedied where they originate. Direct subsidies as income top-up should only be applied in areas of the economy where difference of location or family size have an adverse effect. If this balancing were undertaken by associations, or in other words regulated contractually, the state could increasingly withdraw from the economy so that the economic administration becomes more and more autonomous as it realises its social obligations. It is best placed to do this because it possesses precise insights into specific situations.

Income balancing can be accomplished in either an upwards or downwards direction. If agricultural produce is in short supply, so that even the least favourable locations have to be used, the market price will be governed by the worst production conditions. Then farms in favourable locations can relinquish some of their income. If, on the other hand, there is surplus production, as is the case today in wealthy countries due to political manipulation, market prices will be low and will not provide farmers in poor locations with a sufficient income.

Associations can establish companies to provide services that all need, for instance, relating to transport and circulation of goods. Transport costs differ in central or distant locations. Here too associations need to provide a contractually regulated balance. The task of these associations also includes monitoring the supply of adequate funds to education, research, art and social welfare institutions.

Although the state is active in these areas today, there are many places where too little is done or from which the state increasingly withdraws due to shortage of funds. An intercompany association could immediately initiate much-needed activities in this field.

2.11 The role of law and state in determining income

In the works of Rudolf Steiner we find comments about the tasks of the constitutional state, which may seem to contradict what is said here. In *Towards Social Renewal* he writes:

> The essential thing in all this is that the income drawn by those who are not earners themselves ought not to be determined by economic life itself. On the contrary, economic life should be dependent on what arises in this respect from a sense of justice ... Through the rights and legal state that is separated from economic life, something that is a general concern of humanity, the education and support of those not able to work, will really become such a concern. For in the realm of rights something is at work about which all responsible adults should have a voice.[16]

Steiner says here that the incomes of those who do not earn anything themselves should not arise from economic life. In other words, an awareness of rights, rather than economic forces, should dictate these incomes. In the constitutional state, a sense of justice will come to expression where this state has granted economic life its autonomy so that, in consequence, the former becomes 'separated from economic life'. Today many laws exist which do not express a sense of justice because they have emerged from the democratic power struggle of pressure groups and parties. Economic interests use power (through lobbying and propaganda) to impact on parliamentary decisions and national referenda, especially where the distribution of the financial product is concerned. This means that no truly just decisions are possible today. The state in its modern democratic form is not able to ensure just incomes. Law basically exists to overcome the use of power in all human actions, but today power positions are in fact being created and consolidated through legislation.

As long as this remains the case, we will have to give due scope to justice by other means. Rights can also be established under civil or private law. A community of people can formulate generally valid rules for itself by means of contracts, statutes and by-laws. Everyone freely participates in the signing of a contract, and so unanimity is necessary as a matter of principle. Once rules have been decided, they form the basis for rights protected by law in civil actions. We have to learn increasingly to build up a life of rights from below upwards, rather than leaving this task to the authorities. In the political arena we need do nothing more than to change laws in such a way that they do not prohibit our self-administration. In the quotation above, Steiner does not say that the state should distribute incomes but that, for income distribution, economic life must become dependent on the legal order that arises from a sense of justice. In a public lecture, 'Spiritual Science and the Social Question', also concerned with the division between labour and income, Steiner says:

> Now someone might easily say that if you're asking for people's livelihood to be independent of their work, this ideal is already beautifully illustrated amongst civil servants. The modern civil servant is independent in this sense; the amount he earns is not dependent on what he produces but on what is

considered to be necessary for his livelihood. Fair enough; and yet this objection is hugely mistaken. The point is that every individual must be able, in full freedom, to respect this principle and implement it in actual situations. It is not a matter of realising it by generally imposed edict.[17]

In other words, Steiner's ideal had nothing to do with treating all people like civil servants, who live from state taxes. He was convinced, rather, that economic life itself can become social. In the book *Towards Social Renewal* he writes: 'An economic life that is only shaped by its own structures can protect the weak against the strong.'[18] State taxation as 'compulsory gifts' accord well with the state's obligatory tasks, but income distribution should not be one of these.

An 'unconditional' or 'universal basic income' distributed by the state, which is currently lauded as a move towards separating work and income, stands in opposition to these considerations, and thus directly contradicts efforts for social threefolding. State administration ought not to distribute income but we ourselves should do so in our economic collaboration, through human activity instead of the automatism of state administration. Law must play a part in economic activity insofar as it establishes *rules* according to which available income can be fairly allocated. In arguments for a 'universal basic income' it is said that every person has the right only to a basic income, and it would be the task of each person to augment this with additional income in the same way as hitherto, in economic competition, without resort to issues of justice – in other words without 'economic life being dependent on what arises in this respect from a sense of justice' as Steiner puts it very succinctly in *Towards Social Renewal*.[19] Further comments on law, justice and the State are in subsequent sections.

2. LABOUR AND INCOME

2.12 A living threefold order

The methods and structures described in Sections 2.9 and 2.10 illustrate a clearly threefold structure, but not one in which three neatly distinct areas stand alongside each other. In threefolding it is a matter of properly understanding the interplay of three systems in which every person is involved, as we can certainly practise when we consider income distribution. Taking a just allocation of income, we can make a practical beginning in three areas. Companies that wish to work in a new way can gather their resulting experiences and discuss these with one another. The most important thing is to develop and try out a new methodology and new structures.

The *rules* for *income distribution* belong to the life of *rights.* By using their common sense, all the people involved in any context can in principle agree rights and rules. This is not only true in democratic states but also in contractual agreements insofar as these specify rules. Contracts can only arise where all parties or participants agree, and thus this kind of agreement has the best kind of democratic basis. Income distribution is regulated in the rights sphere, but not enforced by state administration. The contractual agreement gives a legal entitlement. Sharing of profit is not a financial act like a purchase, but an application of justice to the economy.

The *application of rules* in an individual instance belongs to the *cultural and spiritual* sphere. The trusted representatives do not hold their position because some higher authority has appointed them, but they are recognised in their role because they are professionally qualified and have life experience.

Through adjusting production to need, *associative collaboration* between different types of companies creates the basis, in *economic* life, for just income distribution. Market prices play a similar role here to a barometer that records changes and developments in the weather. The latter will however become unusable if the pointer is arbitrarily adjusted.

This summary shows that the social order has three functional systems interacting in a complex way, similar to the organ systems in a living organism. Distinguishing these three systems requires precise and detailed knowledge of each separate sphere. To recognise the interaction of cultural life, state, and economy, is hard since living processes and functions are at work. Therefore in practice this always has to be accompanied by ongoing efforts to carefully discern and distinguish.

Work and income must be separated within the economy. Justice enters into profit distribution (as it does in the market economy to ensure regulated exchange instead of theft and robbery) since contractually agreed legal rights play a role here. By contrast, the application of rules to each individual instance is an activity that depends on individual skills and therefore belongs to the sphere of cultural life. Thus we learn to respect the independence of rights life and cultural life in our daily economic activity. Every company or economic enterprise can make a start with separating labour from income, so that this procedure becomes ever more common in the economy.

2.13 Giving gifts and its importance in economics

If we apply the distinction between purchase money, loan money and gift money both in companies and in the overall economy to the distribution of salaries and wages, we will immediately see that income ought not to be purchase money. Nor, certainly, is it loan money. Is it therefore gift money? What do modern realities have to tell us about this question?

2. LABOUR AND INCOME

Gift money has a very large scope in our monetary relationships, and most of it is administered by the state nowadays. It is allocated to caring for the needy, financing education, and promoting research and, in some countries, to the arts. The state draws the funds for this from taxation, according to statutory rules. Rudolf Steiner spoke of taxes as compulsory gifts – a contradictory but very accurate term. Taxes are not purchase money because we do not directly receive anything for them. We only gain an indirect benefit since taxes serve the general public and we belong to the general public. Nor are taxes loan money, since we cannot ask for them back again. Thus they must be ascribed to 'gifts' in a wider sense.

In principle, giving ought to be a free activity. There *is* such free giving but it has only a shadowy existence, and in many places where it appears, no account is taken of it. It occurs where we give something simply because we wish to, and because we see there is a need for it. The recipient is not obliged to give anything in return, but will be grateful. Real gifts must be such that the qualities of giving and receiving can thrive where they occur. In the economy, exchange and purchase have become the focus of activity, and expand their scope to neighbouring areas to such an extent that the importance of giving is often overlooked. There are people who acknowledge it however, and one of them is Genevieve Vaughan. Born in Texas in 1939, she spent some of her life in Italy. For this important thinker, giving is the fundamental gesture of motherliness, which she regards as the opposite of the male, patriarchal principle of exchange. When we exchange, we only give something if we receive something in return. In her view, people think only of themselves when they exchange things, and the market economy is therefore thoroughly egotistic. Exchange leads to competition, dominance, repression and war. Giving, by contrast, ties people into a community, and leads to peace. Vaughan sharply contrasts these two economic activities.[20]

Even if exchange, purchase and trade often assume ugly forms, the mutuality that comes to expression in them is, after all, something very positive. When I exchange or buy, I wish to meet my needs, but I also want my partner in the exchange to have what they are entitled to, and meet their own needs through me. As such, the mutuality of exchange belongs to the great sphere of fraternity and solidarity. The step from giving to purchasing that occurred historically, and is part of every person's development from childhood to autonomy, allows us an important aspect of freedom. We ourselves choose what we wish to buy, whereas a mother caring for her children has to feel and perceive what they need. Later in life it can happen that we express a wish for something, but never know if the gift we receive will be exactly what we wished for. Instead of setting up an opposition between giving and buying, we ought to see the rightful place of each. This distinction is fundamental to an economic order in tune with the modern human being.

Today, though, giving is largely assigned as a task for the state, so that there is a great lack of freedom in areas where it is not necessary, and therefore seriously impedes our development as modern, free human beings. If we wish to live together in freedom, we will have to increasingly take giving in hand ourselves, and this includes the part of income distribution that the state today either manages or prescribes by law: unemployment benefit, social welfare, child allowance, sickness and invalidity payments, state pension, etc. All these payments are ones we can give to those dependent on them within the economy, not arbitrarily and randomly, but based and regulated according to their need.

In this section I wanted to show that all income distribution ought to be an act of giving, not one of buying. This will become clearer still if we study the three types of money in accounting. In a balance sheet, short-term moneys receivable (creditors) and moneys payable (debtors) are *liquidity*, in other words *purchase money*. Long-term credits and debts, by contrast, are *loan money*. In a profit and loss account, expenses and income are presented as *purchase money*. Profit, on the other hand, is neither purchase money nor loan money. It is the net operating result which we can use by free decision based on our own rationale or appraisal, irrespective of reciprocal payments or repayment obligations. Thus it belongs to the category of *gift money*.

Expenditure:	*Income:*
Purchase money	Purchase money
Overheads	Sale of goods and services
Materials	
Energy	
Administration	
Rent	
Depreciation	
Reserves	
Repayment of debts	
Sundries	
Profit:	
Gift money	
Income of all staff	
Donations to cultural life	
Social welfare	

Types of money in a profit and loss account

If we regard the incomes of all staff in a company as profit distribution rather than 'staffing costs', we remove them from the purchase money realm. We give every staff member the share of the profit which they need, and which we wish to give of our own free will. Income distribution becomes a movement of money without counter-movement, and by this means we detach an individual's work from their income. Income is gift money insofar as individuals do not take it themselves but mutually agree its allocation. To ensure that income distribution is not an arbitrary gift, it has to be contractually regulated. Profit distribution must also cover the income of those who make no economic input, including the old, invalids, orphans, single parents of young children, as well as donations to schools, research institutes and independent artists. All these needs can be met by voluntary but regulated gifts rather than taxation. Contractual regulations are a broad field of great and freely configured diversity. They can relate to profit distribution in companies or, if it is a matter of regular donations, can be agreed between separate individuals and institutions. Gift money can arise at various places in money circulation:

◊ from company profits
◊ from individuals' income
◊ from depreciating old assets

Gift money is entirely focused on consumption. If understood in a broad sense, it provides all people with their livelihood, both those who contribute to production and also 'pure consumers'. Rudolf Steiner coined this term for children, old people and people who cannot work; also for those who work in independent cultural life whom we wish to release from the duty to be economically productive.

3. The Administration of Land by the Cultural Sphere

3.1 Initiatives for a new form of land holding

If we use monetary regulations to ensure that capital assets cannot be increased endlessly, flight into material assets occurs; and these assets are extremely well suited to further speculative increase. Today, too, land prices and share prices play an important role in speculative trade. This generally familiar statement might easily lead us to question the validity of trading in land, property and capital. But if the land and capital markets are abolished, who will administer land and capital? Once again it would be easy to resort to state management: the laws could just be changed and the required bureaucracy established. But state Communism has shown the devastating consequences of doing this. So should we just go back to the free market in land and capital, as happened in eastern Europe after 1989, or is there another solution to the problem? Would it be possible to imagine the cultural sector administering land holdings?

Much has been written about land reform, and numerous theories have been developed. Most are Utopian, presenting a desirable future state. Here, by contrast, we start from particular practical examples already in existence, created by individual initiatives. These examples show new forms of land holding that few are aware of, and that, despite their success, have scarcely ever been described in specialist literature, even by threefold social order authors. It is not just their success that makes these examples noteworthy, but also the ideas they are based on, which will be elaborated below.

Administration of land is firstly a question of rights and justice, since whoever owns the land has the right to manage it and to exclude others from such use. Who should hold this right? There are three possibilities for the actual assignment of land:

1. Land is administered as an economic commodity. This is the prevailing view today. One acquires land either by buying or leasing it, and pays a sum for this, either the purchase price or the rent. This turns land into a commodity.

2. Land can be administered by the state, as was usual in the Communist system. To some extent this also happens in economically liberal countries – one need think only of extensive transport networks.

3. Land can be administered by institutions of the cultural sphere (like schools). This only happens to a small extent today. Since the state, local councils and companies in the cultural sphere can buy and sell land, here too it is a commodity.

Something else is meant when, in his writings on the threefold social order, Rudolf Steiner assigns all land administration to the cultural domain. Here he stands in extreme opposition to the prevailing view; and we have trouble picturing what he means since cultural life has been pushed to the shadowy margins and now is largely administered by the state. We can therefore hardly conceive of an autonomous cultural sphere and its organisation. The following examples are therefore instructive.

3.2 Remer and Barkhoff as pioneers

The first project described here arose from seven years of preparatory study. A group of people in northern Germany around Dr Nicolaus Remer (1906–2001), an agricultural researcher and adviser, made an intensive study of the notion of the 'farm as an individuality' that Rudolf Steiner formulated as an encompassing idea in his agricultural course. This group wished to apply this idea in practice in agriculture, and they also picked up on the idea of the 'pedagogical province' which Goethe developed in his novel *Wilhelm Meister.*

During the 1960s they met with another group around Wilhelm-Ernst Barkhoff (1916–1994), a lawyer in Bochum. This eventually led to the founding of the GLS community bank in 1974.[1] It was clear to Barkhoff from his study of threefolding as Steiner describes it that land should be separated from the circulation of purchase money, and he came up with a suitable legal form to allow this new development. After all, part of a lawyer's daily work is to find solutions for real life situations within the law. Barkhoff saw the interpretation of law as a way of developing it further. At the time he often used to say that a lawyer is freer than a judge in developing new solutions from the law as it stands; and that this, indeed, was his task. He therefore used the legal form of a charitable (non-profit) private limited company as a new kind of trust for land holdings. When Barkhoff and Remer met one another, they found that they agreed about agriculture being both practical and ideal at the same time, and this gave rise to their fruitful collaboration.

Nicolaus Remer, who lived at Bauckhof Farm in Amelinghausen (south of Hamburg), devoted efforts there to practice-based research. He felt it was important that his work should not be carried out in some isolated institute but in relation to specific agricultural operations. Here he drew on the idea of the 'Siamese twins' as Rudolf Steiner had presented this in his Agricultural Course.[2] Steiner wanted farmers to be active colleagues in spiritual-scientific research, rather than just its passive recipients, since research was dependent on practical input. Barkhoff's contact with Remer no doubt contributed to the former including the word 'research' in the name of the new companies he founded.

The first project arose east of Hamburg in the small Holstein village of Fuhlenhagen. The farmer, Carl-August Loss, made a gift of his 84-hectare farm (200 acres) which he had run biodynamically since 1954 to a newly founded charitable (not-for-profit) company whose purpose is to maintain the farm as biodynamic in the long term.[3] (It was incomprehensible to agricultural professionals that a farmer would relinquish his property; and this led to a two-year court case until Schleswig high court approved the gift in 1970). Two further families moved to the farm: Trauger Groh and Christian Lehmann formed a farming cooperative with the previous owner Carl-August Loss. The cooperative took on the tenure. Today a modern building stands on an elevation amidst the fields belonging to it. The farm was given the name Buschberghof, and is run by five farmers as a cooperative partnership without limited liability. Someone who wishes to take responsibility for the work is first employed first for two years, before becoming a member of the cooperative with personal liability. There are arrangements that tie the working capital to the land even when the people involved change. The cooperative structure also guarantees continuity of management whenever individuals leave or join, thus avoiding an abrupt change of tenure.

From the outset the project was partly driven by the idea that more people should live in rural areas. Agriculture can have a wholesome and educational impact on people, and this idea was important already at the preparation stage. It was also informed by Nicolaus Remer's encounter with

Karl König's Camphill movement, and social therapy work began at Buschberghof in 1973. Today, twelve people with disabilities are cared for there, and carers are needed who would not otherwise find employment in a rural district.

Life at Buschberghof is sustained by an organised group of consumers of its agricultural produce. This came about in the following way: in 1986, after leaving Fuhlenhagen, Trauger Groh founded the Temple Wilton Community Farm in New Hampshire as a Community Supported Agriculture venture (CSA). The model was imitated in many places – some 13,000 ventures in North America.[4] In Europe the Buschberghof was the first to adopt this model, and became an example for others.

The Buschberghof produce is not sold. Ninety-two families consisting of 320 people, form an economic community and, depending on each family's means, undertake to pay sufficient to cover the costs of running the farm for one year. The workers at the farm do not know how much each family pays. In a gathering of all the families every June, guidelines are first calculated based on the farm's overall monthly needs, for instance, 60 euros per child, 160 euros for the first adult and 120 for the second. Then each family writes down on a piece of paper how much they will commit to paying. The treasurer adds up the total. If it is too small, the process is repeated until the required sum is reached. Each week the families collect the produce they need from 'their' farm; and the farm tries to produce what the community of families needs by offering a diverse range of foods including bread and dairy products. The whole thing is a modern form of self-sufficiency. The people involved concern themselves with the welfare of their farm, its soil, plants and animals, and distribute among themselves what the farm produces. Giving rather than purchase is practised on both sides. One service is not measured against another but each person receives what they need. The economic community is not a corporate entity. The people are regarded as farm members who draw according to their needs. In 2009 Buschberghof was awarded Germany's Ecological Agriculture Prize for this model.[5]

The transformation of land tenure here shows three important effects:

◊ rural depopulation is halted
◊ a large group of people can connect with agriculture in a tangible way
◊ agriculture is enhanced by economic and educational/ therapeutic aspects and thereby rendered more socially inclusive and complete.

Something similar happened at other farms that will be described here, though in different ways at each location. Around the same time the Bauck family adopted the same model of land tenure for their three farms. In 1969 Edward Bauck transferred management of the farm to his four sons and one daughter. They decided to run the three farms as *one* enterprise, and formed a partnership for this purpose. The Bauck family relinquished private ownership of the land, transferring it to a non-profit (charitable) company, Landbauforschungs-Gesellschaft Sottorf. The statutes of this company require farming on its land to be in accordance with the ideas that Rudolf Steiner presented in his Agricultural Course in 1924. The company does not run the farms itself, but contracts this to an agricultural enterprise. These new measures made Bauckhof attractive to a growing circle of people, and since then two more farms have been bought as well as a processing and a trading company. Bauck produce is known throughout Germany and in many other countries. An existing guesthouse was enlarged and a social therapy facility for young people and adults was established in Stütensen, south of Hamburg.

The Ehlers family also embarked on this transformation of

land tenure for their farm at Hasenmoor, north of Hamburg, Germany. From the outset the connection of agriculture with social work also played a key part in this project. The (new) statutes of the Hasenmoor Agricultural Research Company state that the aim of the enterprise is both research and creating the self-contained agricultural 'individuality' of the farm as a basis for the life of disabled people. Around 1970 the farm took on the task of employing people who had been struggling to overcome drug addiction. Neither the farm nor these people themselves received funding for this. The problems of the latter improved rapidly, and as a result the farm became well known for its therapeutic success, gradually developing its social therapy work with 40 such people. Today the farm is almost unrecognisable from the old days: beautiful modern buildings, a large shop with a café, many people committed to their work. A hundred people work at the farm, sixty also living there. It manages an area of 160 hectares (400 acres).

Two further farms were bought up, one in Weide, the other in Hardebek in the north of Germany. These two farms are independent, with their own agricultural company. Here again the key idea is to create possibilities for people to live in the countryside. Today 65 people in need of care and 40 co-workers live at the Weide-Hardebeck community farm. The legal form is a little different here: the agricultural company is not only the owner of the land but also runs the whole enterprise with both its agricultural and social therapy aspects. This form was chosen so that those responsible for running the enterprise also safeguard its underlying idea. Five people who wish to serve the ethos, and who determine their roles themselves, form the 'management group' and work for the agricultural research company on a remuneration basis.[7]

Dannwisch Farm at Horst, north-west of Hamburg, was converted to biodynamic agriculture by the Scharmer family in 1957.[8] Today it comprises 149 hectares (370 acres).

After long study of the ideas of Remer and Barkhoff, an association was founded in 1986, Verein zur Förderung der Landwirtschaft. The Scharmers gave their land along with the buildings and livestock to the association. The association has 26 members; new members are co-opted in the same way as is done on a board of trustees. A farm community consisting of five families runs the farm. Those responsible for running the operation are at the same time members of the association, whose task is to keep an eye on the overarching ideals of the venture, over and above daily agricultural concerns. Dannwisch Farm has a large circle of customers and friends who benefit from a diverse range of produce. Classes from the Rudolf Steiner School in Hamburg-Nienstedten regularly come to visit and are accommodated in premises that can house up to 40 people. Two buildings were lost in a fire, and one collapsed under the weight of snow, but it was possible to rebuild all three. The farm is continually developing, showing that these new legal forms meet its needs. One area so far seen as unsatisfactory is that of care of the elderly, which can only be sustainably managed by a network of farms together with other business enterprises.[9]

Finally I want to mention Falbringen Farm in Biel, Switzerland, which I managed between 1989 and 2002. Biel City Council, the owner, made this farm available to a private trust on a long-term lease. The trust's aims stipulated that the farm should be run on biodynamic principles, and that it should offer urban schools in the region an opportunity to experience and participate in agricultural work. When a change of leaseholder became necessary, the trust's board had the task of choosing a new leaseholder family. Since the start of the venture, several hundred school classes have been able to benefit from activities at the farm.

3.3 Administering cultural life

The models described here differ from each other in detail but have the same basic idea. New social and legal forms of community were developed from grass roots at each location rather than being dictated from above. A trust or corporate body is appointed as the owner of land. This means that a group of people entrusts management of a farm venture to an agricultural community or a family. Can this be described as land administration by the cultural sphere?

The word 'administration' initially conjures the picture of state bureaucracy whose task is to implement laws decreed by the highest government ministries. The state is a hierarchical organisation, and therefore easily comprehended since it is comparable to a centrally operated machine. Cultural life cannot operate any such form of administration, and in the economy too, administration must assume a different form. Just as interrelated functions in the human organism are not easy to understand, so our thinking is challenged when it tries to grasp the threefold social order. Our abstract, logical thinking always falls back on centralistic concepts if it fails to develop mobile, living ideas.

It is characteristic of the cultural sphere that everything must be based on individual initiative. Rudolf Steiner's idea of cultural life is thoroughly individualistic: 'Spirit can only hold sway amongst people if the spirit is dependent on nothing other than itself, and if all institutions tasked with cultivating the spirit are entirely self-reliant.'[10] We must continually fight for cultural life to remain independent and individual. As soon as it falls into fixed organisational forms, it will sooner or later become tyrannical.

> We must continually preserve our freedom
> in respect to the life of spirit or culture. It
> must therefore only be organised in a free and
> independent way. If we let one generation elaborate

its cultural life in a freer way, and then organise it as it wishes, it will completely enslave the following generation. Cultural or spiritual life must truly be free, not just in theory but in a real, living way. Those living within it have to feel free. Cultural life becomes very tyrannical if it spreads far and wide, for it cannot do so unless some organisational form emerges; and when this happens, the mode of organisation immediately becomes tyrannical. This is why a battle must continually be waged in freedom, in living freedom, against the tyranny to which the life of spirit and culture itself so quickly tends.[11]

We can easily find historical evidence to back up this view. When cultural life was predominant before the Greco-Roman era, the only forms of government were theocratic and despotic ones. We will face a great challenge if we give due scope and place to cultural life – which languishes at present – and wish to avoid these dangers.

Rather than a fixed, hierarchical organisational form, strong emphasis on individual freedom needs to be complemented by free, intensive collegial collaboration rooted in a repeatedly renewed independent decision. We can, for instance, experience this in schools. Every teacher must be self-reliant in standing before their class and teaching it. And yet a school cannot exist if teachers do not work together. Many schools have a headteacher; but good headteachers do not restrict teachers' freedom, instead supporting and coordinating it. In the Waldorf School Rudolf Steiner conceived the teaching staff as a body that, in weekly meetings, took ultimate responsibility for management of the school. Here, therefore, management arises directly from collegial collaboration between independent teachers.[12]

Free collegial collaboration is predicated on the notion that all participants subscribe fully to the shared undertaking, and that they meet regularly to work on the ideals and principles underlying this task. This is work that never ends. Collegial self-administration must start from the premise that every person involved can keep developing and changing; and that, in other words, they are spiritually productive and can create something new in their work. Here we can step beyond our personal limitations with our habits, predilections and disinclinations, and connect in ever better ways with the objective wisdom at work in the world. Especially in the new agricultural projects, new models are so far removed from what is normal nowadays that all involved – whether they have been there for many years or have recently joined the venture – have to keep cultivating their inner, spiritual work to avoid lapsing back into old ways. Cultural or spiritual life must therefore be much stronger and more alive than we usually conceive it. Everything we do has to proceed from the idea we connect with. This ideal is not a limitation but a productive power that can impact even on economic productivity.

A free life of spirit within the threefold social order does not simply mean stating that activities already pursued in education, research or art are now free and independent. Rather, every spiritual, cultural institution must work to free itself from within, and not just once but repeatedly anew. Great demands are placed on cultural life if it seeks to be free; and yet this is necessary if it is to have a wholesome effect in the social organism.

The administration of cultural life therefore begins with every single free initiative which does not shut itself off in isolation but connects with others through collegial discussions, sharing of experiences, coordination and collaboration. For land administration, too, we have to picture development occurring from below; and this, precisely, is the exemplary aspect of the new forms of ownership that have emerged from individual initiatives (see also Section 4.2).

3.4 'Land must be tied to an idea'

This motto was one Nicolaus Remer repeatedly emphasised, highlighting the most important aspect of a real solution to the question of land ownership. If we properly understand the meaning of this phrase, it expresses the first principle which land owners must observe if they wish to relinquish the idea that their land can be *sold* and *inherited*. It points to the only truly new way to embark on lasting land reform. An individually formulated assignment of purpose is needed here for every place on earth, for every plot of land. However, the formulation itself is not enough – the land must also be connected with *living* cultural activity. In other words, people must inwardly sustain this idea by developing and elaborating it for themselves. They themselves take on the task of ensuring that the land is used in accordance with this idea. In our legislative system, the concept of ownership, based as it is on the principle of dominion (*dominium* in Latin), is an obstacle for these new forms. But there is a means to formally constitute them by transferring ownership of land to a corporate body. The corporate body is not the important thing as such, but the fact that a group forms of people who take responsibility for the venture.

The group can transfer use of the land in question to one or more suitable people. This is possible for every type of land use. In agriculture, they must be people who are not only able to run a farm business, but who also understand how to produce food of real benefit to human beings and how to cultivate the soil and landscape in a living, nurturing way. Land used for industrial purposes must also be connected with an idea: it should serve the production of items necessary for and beneficial to humankind. In the case of housing plots, it is a matter of making healthy and beautiful dwellings available. The owners of a villa with a large garden – an imaginary example – could transfer their ownership to a foundation and specify that the property is to benefit families with children. Luxurious isolation is overcome, useful dwellings erected, and the gardens can be used for those who live there to grow their own fruit and vegetables and keep some livestock. There is nothing better for children than a natural environment in which they witness people working purposefully, and are able to join in with this activity.[13]

The idea must be rendered so effective that the managers of a farm business or other venture must also be its active proponents. This is especially important in agriculture since no one can connect as fully with the farm, as enterprise, as they can. Even if this is not so initially, the managers must even, over time, come to be the idea's most important representatives; and then, when it is time to choose successors, they will have a key role and influence. There is also formal provision for this continuity in the farm community since usually members only leave it singly, and new ones are chosen. The controlling company then has a supporting function and should only intervene in an emergency. Today, more than ever, managers are faced with increasing entrepreneurial decisions. Here an idea can only be effective if people assimilate it as an inner impulse. It is useless to enshrine the idea in the statutes as an externally imposed requirement or task. At all farms, developments have shown how important it is to keep alive the idea which initially inspired the work – when new people join a project and as generations change.

Administration of cultural life has nothing centralised about it, but lives from the insights and initiative of the people involved. This applies equally to schools, colleges or universities, research centres, artistic institutes and to the cultivation of religious life. As mentioned in Chapter 2, Rudolf Steiner also assigned criminal and civil court judges to the sphere of cultural life. They should not be organs of the state nor chosen or determined by such organs. The institutions of cultural life can and should work together in a collegial way by sharing experiences and offering each other support. All this needs to be conceived in a far more living way than is usual today – as something founded entirely on each individual's free, independent capacity for development and insight. Land administration must become infused with this living spiritual life. We can begin immediately and anywhere with this if we want.

3.5 Land in public use

If we consider the specific details of land administration, the question arises as to how plots for so-called public use should be allocated. Let us take the park areas in cities as an example. If a population is largely agreed that 20 per cent of an urban area should not be built on, but should serve as green spaces for recreation, this can be determined democratically and enshrined in law. A city council does not have to cultivate or care for these spaces itself but can pass them as gift endowment to charitable organisations that wish to undertake this and can in turn commission a company to do the work. This care of green spaces is a social and cultural task which must be undertaken in every instance by people's free entrepreneurial initiative. The funding for it must be made available as free donations. This will only work if the citizens of an urban area connect far more personally with the public property of parks than they usually do today, when the council levies taxes and individuals can only, at most,

3. THE ADMINISTRATION OF LAND BY THE CULTURAL SPHERE

inspect the accounts to see what percentage of their taxes are being spent on urban recreation areas. This example is relatively straightforward.

The allocation and administration of roads and traffic arteries is more complex, but this too can be governed by the same principles as soon as we have familiarised ourselves a little with how to handle these approaches. It will however then no longer be possible to draw a prospective road or railway line on a map and force this through parliament without the agreement of those involved or affected.

If we try to picture such an approach today, everyone cries out 'Much too complex, unrealisable!' Because we think this, we always prefer centralised methods that we can imagine far more easily; and so very few people nowadays doubt that public areas must be administered by the state and that it should be responsible for the general good.

3.6 The economic value of land

The concept of ground rent is of outstanding importance for the land ownership question. It is said that the financial value of land can be quantified by means of ground rent. The fact that owners can require lease payments for the land is founded on this idea of ground rent. Ground rent is understood as interest on a capital value. By purchasing land, one accumulates financial assets in the land and expects to receive a return equal to that of other capital assets. This gives land a purchase price. The more the price fluctuates, the better is land fitted to be an object of speculation in the land market.

Rudolf Steiner had a different view of ground rent and the financial value of land. He said that land ought to have no price because it is not a commodity, and should not be exchanged for money or any other economic reciprocation.

This would mean an end to the market in land and building plots. No other land reformer of the time expressed this idea in such clear and comprehensive terms. Since then, followers of Steiner have often repeated it; but if we examine what they actually make of these principles in detail, their concepts and recommendations always retain a smaller or larger residue of market ideas. The question therefore arises as to whether one can understand the economic value of land without any recourse at all to prices and markets.

Many economists do not wish to relinquish the commodity character of land since the latter plays a major role in the banking system. The huge amount of credit which the modern economy needs for investment is preferably always given in return for a pledge on real estate. Land and property can serve as security because it can be sold if necessary. Usually however the success of entrepreneurs is the real security since there is, after all, always an expectation that they will repay the loan with interest. Mortgages only provide an apparent security which can be replaced by other methods in banking (further details in Chapters 4 and 5).

Even if land has no price, it does have an economic value. A fertile soil in a favourable climate is more valuable for agricultural productivity than a poor meadow on a steep mountain slope. Ground rent should therefore reflect this *real value*. In this context Rudolf Steiner criticised general education:

> It really is high time today for people to realise that to be an educated person it is not sufficient to know that three times nine equals twenty-seven. They should also know what the thing called 'ground rent' actually is. I'd like to ask you how many people today have any clear idea of what ground rent really is.[14]

In economics textbooks, ground rent is usually defined in accordance with market economy ideas, for instance, 'Rent is the income derived from the ownership of land and other natural resources in fixed supply' (www.britannica.com). It is correct of course that the supply of land is inelastic, since land cannot be produced or multiplied. The more people rent or buy land, the less of it there is available, and the higher the rental or purchase price becomes unless the state intervenes. In every market, after all, a kind of power struggle takes place between suppliers and purchasers. In the case of land, suppliers are in a stronger position because many people wishing to buy or rent are competing with each other. Those renting will accept price increases as long as they still regard the rent as manageable. Something similar applies to purchase price: purchasers consider whether the ground rent and rental sum they obtain for the land, with all possible price increases, will enable them to obtain as high a return on their capital as other capital investments.

If ground rent is defined in this way, it is an outcome of market contest, and thus a price. Is this price founded on the same kind of value as commodities and services? A recent textbook states: 'Land as such does not yet have any economic value.'[15] But then the author continues: 'The more suited the land is for the production and sale of goods, for tourism and the rent of offices and dwellings, etc., the higher will the ground rent be.' But this means nothing other than that land becomes valuable when something is done with it. Only then does it provide a ground rent.

Can one ascertain the level of this ground rent? Where exactly the same amount of work and the same capital expenditure is assigned to two different pieces of land of diverse kinds, the yield can be very different in each case. This is true not only of agricultural usage but also of any other. The difference is due to the land, location, road connections, etc.

The overall sum that any piece of land can yield therefore consists of three parts: one arising from labour, one assignable to capital, and one produced by the land itself, that is, the ground rent. But now we have to ask how high each of these is, especially the ground rent, and where does it appear? Theoretical calculations often proceed by subtracting labour costs and capital costs from the total income. Labour costs are determined by wages, thus the 'labour market', and capital costs by the capital market. The ground rent is indirectly determined as remainder after costs, and represents profit that can be garnered from the land or plot. It is then said that this profit, this ground rent, belongs to the owner of the land.

On the other hand, unused land itself also has a price, the level of which is determined by the interplay between supply and demand. The two values cannot be computed together, but both can be attributed to the fact that we seek to put a monetary figure on the value of land and ground rent. This seems to be the basic error. There are pieces of land which produce no ground rent that can be calculated in monetary terms, despite the fact that they are certainly not useless. If, say, people on a piece of land work as much and as inventively as possible but still only just survive, the ground rent viewed as capital interest is equal to zero, no rent can be obtained from the land and it cannot be considered as a capital asset. This does not mean the plot is worthless however, for it may certainly be productive at a low level.

Steiner goes on in the lecture quoted above to explain the concept of land value with a formulation one can feel to be complex and elaborate:

> In relation to the overall economy land is worth
> so and so much according to its productivity, or
> in other words according to the manner or degree
> of its rational exploitation. For people today it is
> very difficult to think of this simple land value in
> clear terms, because in a modern economy interest
> or capital in general has become confused with
> ground rent. This is because the real economic

value of ground rent has been falsified by mortgage
law, bonds and stocks trading, and suchlike. In
consequence everything has basically been distorted
by impossible, untrue ideas. Naturally we can't
therefore suddenly gain a real idea of ground rent.
But we should think of ground rent simply as
the economic value of the land in relation to its
productivity.

This clearly states that the value of the land is not a
product, but a productivity value; that is, a production factor.

3.7 Non-monetary values

Steiner thus seeks the concept of an economic value for land
that cannot be expressed in monetary terms. We have already
characterised this concept of value in the section on labour
and earnings. But we are so used to thinking of economic
values in terms of prices that it is hard for us to shed the
habit. People think they will have no safe ground to stand on
if they cannot record a value in figures. We conceive of the
income of a piece of land as return on the capital we invested
in it when we purchased it. As long as we are stuck on this
idea, we will always define land as a purchasable commodity.
Return on capital, lease payments and rent are all seen in
terms of interest, and we conceive of interest as a price
whose amount is determined by market economy forces. In
Chapter 2 we saw that, as production factors, land, labour
and capital stand outside the market economy and precede
it chronologically. Production factors have nothing to do
with an exchange process between finished outputs, but they
facilitate the one-sided process of production and output.

The value of land cannot be calculated in monetary
figures. Nevertheless it can be clearly recorded by describing

it. The value of a plot of land consists, for instance, in the fact that one can engage in agricultural production on it and can achieve precisely determined yields from this. The value of a different parcel of land will be valued for the construction of industrial facilities or dwellings because of its location near traffic routes. These value descriptions show clearly that the means of production offer opportunities for economic activity, not finished products.

3.8 Reform ideas in the nineteenth century

In Rudolf Steiner's day, various land reform ideas were afoot. Here I will consider two important ones, whose fundamental principles repeatedly resurfaced at later periods.

The American Henry George (1839–1897) regarded private income earned from land ownership as the root of all social injustice, and enquired into how economic returns are distributed across the three production factors of labour, land and capital. He considered the proportion of income received from labour and capital to be justified, but appropriation of ground rent to be unjust, and suggested that this should entirely absorbed into state taxation in the form of a 'Single Tax' which he believed could replace all other taxes. His book, *Progress and Poverty*, published in 1879, was widely read in America at the end of the nineteenth century. However, nowhere did the 'one-tax movement' make any headway. In Europe it was suppressed by Marxist socialism, which demanded that the state should appropriate land without offering payment for it.

Silvio Gesell (1862–1930), a German merchant and economist, sought to abolish capital speculation and land speculation simultaneously. With his proposals for a 'natural economic order', he suggested that the state should appropriate all land, paying compensation for it, and then lease it again to the highest bidders. Market laws would, he thought, ensure that rent amounts evened out to the level of ground rent. But Gesell also recommended that ground rent estimates should be carried out regularly every three, five or ten years, His concern was that all ground rent should flow into state coffers. This was likewise to apply where building land was transferred via heritable building rights in which the person with a right to build is the owner of the buildings and sells these when he passes on the land. From rental incomes, the state would be able to fund compensation for land appropriation, and in this way it would eventually redeem all the land. Once all compensation has been paid off, money from ground rent should be given to mothers so that they could feed and raise their children without being dependent on their men. Gesell tested his ideas in diverse contexts which he carefully examined and described in vivid language. It is still worth reading his original texts.

George and Gesell both retained the ground rent but allocated it to the state rather than to private landowners.

3.9 Did anyone understand Rudolf Steiner?

It is at this point that Rudolf Steiner (1861–1925) joined the debate, with his far more revolutionary ideas. He integrated land into his concept of the threefold social organism, stating that land should not be administered in the economic sphere because economics creates a market for everything. The market is the natural and right distribution principle of the economy, which renders everything a commodity and allocates everything a price. Since ownership of land is not a commodity but a right of use, the foundations of land administration must be created in the rights sphere. Land principally belongs to all people because they all have an equal right to live on the earth. But since they do not wish to and cannot all make equal use of it, all those involved or affected must together agree rules for allocation of land. Determining these rules is a matter of justice, in the rights domain. But in actually allocating land in each case individual capacities and needs must be assessed, and this is a task for the cultural sphere. In each instance, land must be distributed according to legally determined rules so that it benefits those who make good use of it as an economic production factor. Two preconditions must be met by users of land: the professional, specialist expertise needed in each case, and the will to use these for the good of humanity.

Students and followers of Steiner have taken many of his ideas, updating and elaborating them. Udo Herrmannstorfer has engaged with them in an especially thorough way.[16] We will summarise his thoughts insofar as they apply to our present theme. Hermannstorfer assumes that the new order of land rights should be undertaken by a change in law, and will apply to the whole land area of a country from the day such a law comes into effect. Accordingly, land will become unsellable. 'Land and property are handed over to society for this purpose' (p. 52). One could also say that land's purchasability would no longer be a part of ownership rights, as it is today, for society too could not sell land any more. Land ownership is not abolished in this view, but henceforth has another meaning: it becomes a comprehensive but time-limited right of usage. General expropriation of land will allow the previous owner to automatically become the owner in line with this new meaning:

> Further transfer of ownership can be effected
> in each case by the previous owners themselves.
> A social entity that administers land will only
> intervene where no first user has yet been appointed
> (undeveloped land) or where previous owners have

not themselves determined a successor; or where overriding social perspectives have to be asserted.

Unlike land on which houses stand, houses themselves can be sold: 'The right usage of land automatically follows property rights on buildings, which – in contrast to the land – can be sold and purchased' (p. 52). Compensation for expropriation involves the reimbursement of expenses actually incurred if these were permissible in law at the time. Only such expenses elicit compensation, and not the land's current market value.

Herrmannstorfer also endorses a usage charge payable by someone who is granted use of a piece of land. But the amount of the charge should not, as proposed by Gesell, be determined by market laws, but instead be in line with reasonable social ones. This can and will lead to a strong impact on social conditions, benefiting agriculture, multi-family housing and charitable institutions. Economical handling of land should be rewarded. Undeveloped building land will not be hoarded over long periods because these charges must be paid and unused land will be expensive. 'In special cases it would be possible to have the user fee given to the highest bidder in a public invitation to tender' (p. 54). Here, in this specific instance, Hermannstorfer links up with Silvio Gesell's proposals, according to which land distribution is determined by market forces. The land involved could be plots that have not previously had users.

The usage charge, according to Hermannstorfer, should benefit those who need social welfare support and suchlike. This is attributable to the fact that land belongs to all people but that not all can make equal use of it. This assigned purpose means that the land usage charge would replace a portion of taxation needed for social welfare.

Who would administer land distribution? Hermannstorfer proposes public legal entities, whose citizen representatives would be democratically authorised in separate elections. These entities would contrast with local council administration by their status as citizen self-administration institutions.

Christoph Strawe, who has taken up Hermanstorfer's proposals, argues as follows: 'But since every form of use at the same time excludes others from using this same piece of land, the demand for equality requires the compensation payment of a justly assessed usage amount.' Here, therefore, land use is still paid for in money, and has a price for the user.

After East Germany, the German Democratic Republic, ceased to exist in 1989, the *Seminar für freiheitliche Ordnung* (Free Social Order Seminar) sent proposals to 6000 local councils in the region, suggesting that land should not be sold but endowed as legal heritable building right.[18] Ground rent should be absorbed entirely by resulting leasehold payments. In relation to already existing private land ownership, the seminar suggested that the West German parliament should likewise fully replace ground rent with land taxes. When the land no longer produces an interest-like return, its capital value declines to zero, so that it cannot any longer be sold. These proposals are based on the market economy definition of ground rent and envisage a change of law to withdraw ground rent from private users.

In the reform proposals referred to here, the details are varied and noteworthy. But common to all of them, also those of students and followers of Rudolf Steiner, is the fact that they seek to withdraw ground rent from landowners, and to do so by means of state legislation. Anyone who then wishes to use land has to pay a usage charge or fee, very similar to the way a tenant must pay rent. In other words, these measures do not abolish the price of land but instead more or less siphon it off and allocate it to all of society.

3.10 Redemption of land with usage fees

There is an initial advantage with this approach: capital is accumulated with which land can increasingly be redeemed. Private institutions can do this as well as the state. One such is the Edith Maryon Foundation active in Switzerland, Germany and other countries.[19] This started in 1990 and is the owner of many agricultural, commercial and housing properties which it leases out to groups of people who are, as far as possible, self-administering. In Basle, six full-time staff work for the Foundation, managed by Christoph Langscheid, one of the founders. In Berlin the Foundation has six properties leased by Allmendia GmbH. In the case of housing, the Foundation does not rent out premises in the usual way but instead tenants take on ownership rights and duties. To do so they have to organise themselves by forming housing associations. They take care of repairs and renovations, and where possible suggest new tenants whom they themselves choose. The rental fee is not decided by the housing market in isolation but is based on real costs. In addition a 'usage fee' is charged, and calculated as part of the rent so that capital for new projects can be created. The tenants are willing to pay this usage fee as long as the rent remains comparable to that in the rest of the housing market. The Edith Maryon Foundation is one example of other, similar undertakings.

Redemption of land is in theory meaningful until the point where all land has been redeemed or given away. Redeeming land is of benefit for the pieces of land affected and the people who use them. However, those who sell the land acquire capital assets that would be better spent to benefit cultural and social ventures. It is different when the land is simply given away so that inappropriate ownership is voluntarily relinquished and allows the creation of new types of legal relationship. But this depends on personal decisions of an altruistic nature.

It is correct to say that usage ownership introduced through new land legislation would be easy to implement. This would give opportunities to the best entrepreneurs. There would be a market economy variant to facilitate their choice whereby the usage fee is set at a high enough level to ensure it covers all operationally achievable ground rent. This will be the case if one leases the land to the highest bidder, as Silvio Gesell proposed. But application of the market economy principle can also be limited if the municipality, for instance, chooses contenders according to other perspectives. However, as long as there is a usage fee, a residue of market economy still applies. For the user, the usage fee is a cost factor by means of which ground rent is siphoned off.

Authors who wish to follow Rudolf Steiner in making land altogether unpurchasable, regard the usage fee as a long-term solution of the land question. Eckhard Behrens, for instance, a legal expert close to the Free Social Order Seminar, writes:

> It is economically feasible to entirely remove land's capital value by withdrawing ground rent from landowners ... access to land would be more readily available if capital expenditure were no longer needed for this. It would however require the person acquiring the land to be able to generate a charge of the same amount as ground rent. Why? Well, no one ought to hoard land in future, and therefore the charge must also be paid if one fails to use it or does so in an inadequate way. Anyone who makes good use of the land will have the necessary income to pay the rent, and thus land will migrate to the best user of it. This is desirable in the economy as a whole. And it also best serves the common interest, since, due to scarcity of land, it should be managed in the best possible way.[20]

This argument is also entirely based on market economy ideas. In relation to current land purchasing, economists likewise state that the market will ensure that land reaches the best user.

3.11 Ground rent in the distribution of economic return

Land ownership plays a role for many people in relation to old age provision. Farmers who own a farm, for instance, assume that they will sell this when they're old and live from the proceeds. If a farmer gives his farm away, his care in old age must be ensured by some other means. And here we should free ourselves entirely from the idea that care of the elderly should be dependent on the assertion of ownership entitlements. It is a fiction to accumulate assets for one's old age. Just as one cannot care in advance against one's own illness or accident, so there is no such thing as advance provision for old age. Whoever is economically productive now must at the same time provide for people who cannot be so. Someone who is old and draws a pension is being fed and cared for by those able to do this. No directly connected give-and-take is involved here, but rather a unilateral, benevolent giving, and an equally unilateral, grateful receiving. In other words, care of the elderly involves acts of giving. Our modern insurance system conceals the reality that insurance instalments are not paying for one's own illness or losses but only for those of others that occur right now. All insurance should be reformulated as a legally organised economy of giving.

What does ground rent have to do with this? Steiner repeatedly emphasised that ground rent always arises and cannot be eradicated by any measure such as taxation. If this is true, then it is important to determine how and for what purpose this rent is used. What is it there for? Can it be used to support people who are unable to work? Initially we can see that the part of net financial yield not used by working people and their families is available for the unemployed. This excess part of the economic product has a 'benefit' character and makes giving possible. Here therefore we are not concerned with where this benefit originates, as for example in the terms 'ground rent' or 'capital return', but with *usage* of the rent or benefit, its giving or endowing character. (The German *Rente* means both 'rent' as in ground rent, and 'pension' or 'benefit'.) Nowadays the state finances large portions of social expenditure through taxes and deductions, and thus through 'gifts' enforced by legislation.

Every social benefit payment, as a value stream flowing in only one direction, has the character of a gift. With all benefits one can either focus on where they come from and what funds them, or instead on the recipients. Ground rent and government bonds (bond loans) tell us where the income originates that can be claimed without quid pro quo. By contrast, old age and invalidity pensions tell us *who* benefits. Origin and target group are logically distinct in the case of every benefit. In the case of ground rent, too, therefore, we must distinguish between its origin and the purpose it serves.

◊ Ground rent's origin is described as follows: Ground rent is the yield of the land as production factor that one cannot calculate in monetary terms.

◊ Ground rent's usage can be described as follows: Ground rent is contained in the economic product and helps to facilitate the financing of all incomes, especially those of people who are 'pure consumers', i.e. children, single mothers, the sick, elderly and invalids; and all who work in the independent cultural life.

The land provides food, clothing, accommodation, etc. to these people, however, only if it is managed or cultivated.

The earth belongs to all humankind, and so all have an entitlement to this product since the profit includes ground rent in an indistinguishable combination with the yield of labour and capital. Distribution of profit, as we saw in Chapter 2, is not a sale involving service and payment, but a process in one direction. Distribution of profit is accomplished according to criteria different from those governing its origin, and requires a new act of will. This can be freely determined yet not be random as long as detailed rules are first elaborated and then applied in each individual instance. Thus ground rent can vanish without trace in the profit sum and, in profit distribution, be allocated to all consumers according to need criteria. By means of this kind of profit distribution, support of those who cannot work themselves loses its 'alms' character. Their need is recognised and acknowledged as a legal entitlement as much as that of all those who are economically productive.

Here we can recall our comments on administration of land by the cultural sphere. We achieve true social community when the land is connected with ideal goals and tasks. Then the user does not have to be compelled by charges to make over the ground rent for the common good, but instead it becomes possible for the whole body of co-workers to voluntarily implement purposeful social rules in relation to profit distribution.

In the interim, transitional period, we can certainly use the siphoning off of ground rent by the state as a tactical strategy since in many cases people have to learn to think in new ways, and they often do not achieve their goals by direct means. But this measure alone cannot be a lasting solution to the land question. At the same time, land administration by the cultural sphere must gradually be developed from the grass roots upwards. If we wish to bring about land reform by nothing other than the siphoning off of ground rent, this is to embark on a path without any spiritual foundation or exertion. The other path, which connects the land with an idea, starts from spiritual, mental exertion. State legislation and politics can never give rise to this. Their chief task is to not inhibit free initiatives, in this domain too. All renewal and progress must today start with ourselves. We ourselves must take responsibility for things that are not the task of the state, creating new, appropriate structures in economic and cultural life outside of state governance. This is a path towards threefolding of the social organism which accords with our modern era. It starts in the life of spirit and culture and from there leads into the realm we today refer to as the private economy or private sector.

4. Capital and the Means of Production

4.1 Natural and legal persons

Nowadays there are small enterprises in which individuals or 'natural persons' as they are known in law, bear independent entrepreneurial responsibility as owners of a business. They obtain credit as personal loans and pledge their private assets as security for the debts of their company. This applies not only to sole traders but also to partnerships. But most companies, and almost all large ones, are limited liability companies, trusts, associations, etc. and are what is called a 'legal person' (contrary to a 'natural person'). Here the company will be run by company employees who are not personally liable for its losses and debts. They can only be held accountable for personal negligence. Managers, the board of directors, etc. are answerable to the company's owners (shareholders in a limited company) who can elect and also dismiss them. In a limited company, the funders are not creditors but owners and partners. Instead of interest they receive a dividend, a share of the profit. As owners they determine the company 'strategy' and, if they pursue their own interests, wish first and foremost to ensure high profits. All this became possible when the idea of the 'legal person' was invented.

The concept of the legal person first developed in the nineteenth century. At the time of the French Revolution, only natural persons were acknowledged as having legal economic competency. During the nineteenth century joint-stock companies in America, and then also in Europe, acquired equal status with natural persons, and were thus able to become the owners of means of production and capital, to conclude contracts and to be liable for adherence to them. Since then we have become so accustomed to this idea of the legal person that it is hard for us to conceive of a legal and economic order without this fiction.

Yet Rudolf Steiner believed that 'In future a certain concept will have to disappear entirely – the idea of the legal person and also of the economic-legal person,'[1] since the legal or juristic domain is concerned with inter-personal relations, with relationships between people as human beings. This is only possible between 'natural persons', whether as separate individuals or groups. Means of production and capital can be personally made available to such people if they have the appropriate capacities. Steiner repeatedly stressed that credit could only be given to individuals. A right of use should enable entrepreneurs to dispose of productive capital in the greatest freedom:

> To administer the total amount of capital in such a way that specially gifted individuals or qualified groups can get the use of it to apply it as their particular initiative prompts them, must be to the true interests of everybody in a community. Everybody, intellectual or labourer, must say (if they steer clear of prejudice and consult their own interests): I not only wish an adequate number of persons, or groups of people, to have absolutely independent use of capital, but I should also like them to obtain this capital through their own initiative. For they themselves are the best judges of how their particular abilities can make capital a means of producing what is useful to the body social.[2]

Free disposal of capital and means of production is guaranteed today by the right of ownership. Capitalist theories like to stress that the state's principal task is to protect private ownership. These theories generally do not distinguish between entrepreneurial access to the means of production, or the passing on of the latter through sale or inheritance. Here we need to review the concept of ownership (see Section 4.5). Prevailing capitalist theory combines in the ownership concept things that are both correct and erroneous. A company management needs to have free access to capital: this is a wholesome state of affairs, whereas the inheritance and sale of capital assets is harmful. The right of use, as threefold ideas see it, aims to strengthen this free availability and disposal but, in contrast to modern ownership law, only for as long as entrepreneurs exercise it themselves. As many instances demonstrate, this could be done under our current laws. However, people usually have no other choice than to use the legally available company forms and to re-interpret them in their own internal ways. This is not straightforward since legal company forms were conceived for specific purposes, and do not entirely accord with the new aims of economic solidarity.

Lawyers and legal experts can creatively refashion these companies, as Wilhelm-Ernst Barkhoff so ably showed. Nowadays people behave as though associations, foundations, cooperatives and joint-stock companies themselves – and not human beings – were working as 'legal persons', represented and administered by employed managers. Internally, however, one can see these companies in a way that allows those with prime responsibility to be, for all practical purposes, elevated to the position of autonomous entrepreneurs. Even in a joint-stock company it is possible to grant the directors full autonomy if the absolute majority of voting shareholders lies not with private owners but with an association or foundation, and if the latter is conceived so that the association or foundation is always in the control of the respective directorship.[3]

4.2 Administration of capital by the cultural sphere

All productive enterprises depend on being able to invest capital. In small businesses, entrepreneurs often put their own private assets into the company. Since the huge industrial developments in the nineteenth century, however, most businesses have capital needs that cannot be covered by their own private means. We must therefore ask how a board of directors as described above can gain access to the capital needed, and how this should be administered. Nowadays capital is raised by the sale of shares or borrowed against interest payments; in other words, it is administered within the economy. In the capital market it has a price: a business acquires capital if it promises to pay interest or dividends. Share capital can also produce capital gains and losses in speculative finance markets. All these gains are only possible because capital is invested in the productive economy, and the economy is dependent on this to the degree that it actually needs capital. But today assets increase so greatly through speculative gains that owners of these assets continually seek further investment opportunities, causing the economy to invest more than is really necessary.

State debt is also very much in the interests of the owners of large assets. The destructive nature of this immoderate economic growth is well-known; but it cannot be remedied as long as administration of capital is left with the capital market. It is said that the capital market ensures that capital is directed to where it is needed. If the capital yields profit, it is assumed that it has been used in an economically productive way – that there are no further concerns and it is sufficient to chase profit. Market economy theory therefore declares profit to be a positive force, and denies human beings any further responsibility in the matter.

Responsible capital administration must replace the capital market, both for monetary and real capital (means of production). State administration is unsuitable for doing this since it inhibits free initiative. Rudolf Steiner was already aware of this in his day, as the 'experiment' of Communism was just getting underway in Russia. There is no other means to do this than by organising all capital administration so that the free initiative of skilled people can come into effect. For this, structures are needed to be administered by the cultural life, as have been described earlier for land administration. While this is something very practical and not Utopian, as we saw in the last chapter, there is fundamental resistance to it because people have little trust in cultural life, and do not believe it can work successfully in this domain. Autonomy is not assigned to cultural or spiritual life since the spirit is regarded as something secondary, as a property and effect of matter. Thoughts are only considered valid if they are confirmed in a material experiment. The life of spirit is not only kept unfree externally, by the state, but also from within by humankind's materialistic outlook. A free life of spirit and culture must be developed from within, and this work must go hand in hand with external acknowledgment of its autonomy and independence.

As described in the last chapter, one major difficulty is that we have no clear idea what 'administration by the cultural sphere' would look like. Ideas already outlined there lead us to ask how, through cultural life which is organised in a very individualistic rather than centralised way, we can administer the economy's productive capital. 'Individualistically organised' means that every company will approach things in a distinct and different way. Assuming an enterprise that is already furnished with real capital and is running a successful business with it, we can see that when the company directorship changes because someone leaves, the method for appointing new board members can differ in each company. In all cases, though, the following two principles are important: freedom of the individual and collegiate collaboration that complements and creates a context for this. People successful in their work who leave, as well as those who remain company directors, are well placed to have a say in the choice of new managers or directors.

In addition to avoid isolation, every enterprise needs a supervisory board composed of professionals who can come from very varied fields of society and whose task is to be aware of how the company is run and to keep checks on it. First and foremost they need to keep an eye on the company's original ideals and purpose, and safeguard this against the profit motives of external funders. While the funders will be kept fully informed, they should have no power to decide company management appointments since it is not their task to ensure that the company meets its financial obligations. The directors themselves do this.

Similar principles must also be applied when providing a company with new financial capital for investments. Here company initiative is the most important factor, and this should not be restricted because profit perspectives lead banks and rating agencies to evaluate the company's credit-worthiness from a one-sided perspective. Funders must be concerned with quite different questions, such as, do we wish to support the aims of the company because we regard them as useful and beneficial? Do its objectives serve the common good, and do we trust the directors to realise their aims?

Today, already, many savers want to know what their money is being used for, and are less concerned with the amount of profit they make. Alternative banks have much experience of their clients' wishes in this respect, and other banks must adapt to this a little. In such questions we ourselves, as owners of capital, must become competent decision-makers when we wish to invest our funds. Transparent information is required for this, and good contact between company and funders. The entrepreneur is best placed to judge whether his projects are useful and will produce a yield. However, he cannot make isolated decisions about this, but should instead ensure that those who provide the necessary credit understand and acknowledge his intentions. In contrast to the words 'approve' or 'permit', which stress the will aspect, the word 'acknowledge' expresses the fact that insight and understanding are involved. We can put it like this: we ourselves would not have thought of a venture, but we understand it now, and therefore we support it. In this sense the company must find a circle of people who wish to support its aims.

4.3 Acknowledging entrepreneurial initiative in cultural life

What has been described shows that a principle characteristic of cultural life – and one we discussed in Section 3.3. – applies to the forming of company capital. This principle is as follows: Individual initiative and collegiate connection with others who understand the initiative. Rudolf Steiner elaborated this principle with especial clarity in 1923 when he re-founded the Anthroposophical Society in Dornach. When reporting these developments in Prague, he stated:

> You see, anthroposophy can really only work in full freedom if this work meets with understanding everywhere. Anthroposophic activity cannot work as hierarchical intervention, despite the fact that it is inevitably dependent on initiative. This is why, at the conference in Dornach, we so strongly emphasised the fact that the Executive Council formed there seeks to be one of *initiative* and not of administration.[4]

Steiner was speaking here of initiative in the sphere of *free* spiritual-cultural life. In contrast to this, entrepreneurial activity in the economy is practically *applied* spiritual life; but it too depends on initiative, and the forming of company capital is a matter for this sphere. Company directors will cultivate understanding and acknowledgment from their capital providers through regular collaboration with them, for instance in annual meetings where, besides presentation of the accounts, the aims and projects of the company are discussed. Companies with a social impetus or ecological intent already do this today. The principle of initiative and acknowledgment leads in the cultural sphere to collaboration within a free, individualistic form of organisation. The same individualistic principle of cultural life is practically applied to the economic management.

Economic practice according to threefold perspectives is fundamentally different from most current practice. Nowadays over-arching (strategic) issues are decided by proprietors. In threefolding, by contrast, company directors and possibly a supervisory organ are responsible for this, and together they both administer the cultural or spiritual sphere in the company. This spiritual sphere involves directorship, both technical and entrepreneurial, realised in purchases, sales, rationalisations and investments, etc. Physical work is never without a spiritual or intellectual aspect either, but requires skill, reflection, foresight and planning. Rudolf Steiner describes as follows the scope of the spiritual sphere within the social organism:

> In speaking of the threefold social organism, I include not only a more or less abstract life of culture or spirit in the spiritual domain, but also everything that depends on human spiritual or physical capacities. Let me expressly emphasise this, for otherwise one might completely misunderstand the limits of the spiritual sphere in the threefold

social organism. Someone who does only manual work also needs certain skills to do so, and various other capacities, and therefore cannot be regarded as involved in merely economic activity but participates in the spiritual sphere.[5]

This cultural or spiritual sphere must be cultivated in every business outfit. According to modern business textbooks, the overarching aim of a company is to maximise profit – defined as the excess income after covering costs. In future this overriding aim should instead be formulated as the production or provision of something that supports the common good of humanity. The second aim will be to enable the people working in the company to live well from its income, and not simply to be treated as a cost factor. None of this contradicts the maximisation of profit or income but in fact enhances it as a factor necessary to ensure the livelihood of all co-workers; however, it should come second in importance to the primary aim. A third objective will be for a company's products or services to be offered at a fair price. This is particularly important for companies in a monopoly position, such as water or electricity providers, or providers of public transport and communication. In these areas of the economy it is not a question of an alternative between state-run operations or competition. The third and freest solution is that of a business operation with ideal aims. If it is possible to realise these, there will be no need to create competition artificially. People think this is necessary today, even though it often hinders efficient business.

We gain a mistaken view of threefolding if we think that economic life simply consists of a totality of business operations. The truth is, rather, that commercial businesses are active in economic production but must also develop their own cultural sphere and their legal structures.

4.4 The productive value of fixed assets

Production sites or real estate, machines, vehicles and equipment figure as assets in company balance sheets. New international balance-sheet regulations originating in Anglo-American practice, require fixed assets to be assigned their market value, or in other words valued at the amount they could be sold for at the time the balance sheet is drawn up. This is done in the interest of investors, who wish to know the potential stock-market value of a company. Rudolf Steiner's recommendations run contrary to this. As we saw in Chapter 3, he thought that land should never have a market price because it should not be bought and sold but administered in the cultural domain. It therefore cannot be recorded in the balance sheet as a saleable asset. This could already be important to companies that wish not to sell their real estate as a matter of principle. Balance sheet regulations must still of course be observed.

The means of production are a different matter – things that must be manufactured such as premises, machinery, etc. – for they have a procurement price. In his course on economics, Rudolf Steiner spoke of a 'measure whereby the means of production lose their value once they have become means of production'.[6] This surely means that they lose their sale value, for they retain a productive value, and it is the latter that can serve external capital funders as security. The external capital recorded as liabilities is balanced against the value of production facilities that have originally been procured by outside capital. In line with a threefolding perspective, plant and equipment do not represent a value that can be transformed into money through sale. Production facilities are economically productive but are transferred to the sphere of cultural life. Steiner made the following remark in this regard: 'The means of production, insofar as they can be capitalised ... belong in the spiritual sphere of the social organism.'' How should we understand this? What does 'capitalised' mean here?

We all know this term from the realm of interest calculation. If there is a regular interest income, the capital can be calculated from the interest rate. Thus one can capitalise every regular income, including the income from the productivity of production facilities. The capital thus calculated should be administered in the cultural sphere, and therefore has no realisable sale value. But if, despite this – because it is practical – one records the depreciating procurement value of fixed assets according to specific rules, this is not a diminishing market value but an expression of the productivity through which outside funding can gradually be repaid. The more carefully we think through these details, the clearer we can recognise how economic life and cultural life are not separate from each other but connected as distinct parts of a whole organism. Our habitual modes of thought today militate very strongly against this new outlook. To gradually change them will probably only be possible by learning through practical examples to increasingly understand the principles at work here.

If, without considering productivity, we record fixed assets on their original procurement price, and then deduct the depreciation allowance from this, we are thinking of the past. For owners, especially shareholders, the current market value of a company is important. Instead, productivity should look ahead towards the future. Only this future aspect of productivity is a useful counterbalance to external capital. In the case of loan money, too, we are only concerned with the future, specifically with asking whether the company will be in a position to cover agreed regular repayments and interest. Nowadays credit-providers consider not just productivity but also property securities, to protect themselves means against the consequences of a bankruptcy. The provision of credit is always linked to a certain risk by virtue of the fact that it provides entrepreneurs with opportunities to develop their business. If an enterprise founders despite careful planning, the company does not have to be liquidated but can instead look for suitable people to take it further. Credit should of course only be provided for projects which are worth continuing into the future.

4.5 Distinguishing two types of ownership

The concept of private ownership, which we have taken over from Roman law, states that I can do what I will with my property. Nowadays we speak of the social obligations connected with ownership, but find it hard to envisage anything specific in this idea because we do not distinguish clearly enough between things we use in our private life such as our bed and clothes, and ownership of economic means of production (land, buildings, machines, vehicles). Things in our private use are ones we can use, and also sell or bequeath. Both rights of disposal are protected under property law. But in the case of the means of production, by contrast, as we have already described, a clear distinction and division must be made between these two rights of disposal. In accordance with social threefolding there must be a time-limited usage ownership which is available to us only for as long as we make productive use of the property and facilities in question. We can never sell or bequeath them like private possessions, thereby appropriating their value for our private consumption.

Rudolf Steiner puts it like this:

> Nowadays people throw this all into a single pot: businesses founded on capital and the private ownership of capital. But we have to ask whether these two things can be separated? You see, the private administration of business operations,

founded on greater or lesser individual human
capacities, and requiring the aid of capital to be
effective, cannot be rescinded ... But the private
ownership of capital, ownership of private capital,
is something different ... When someone acquires
or has acquired private capital, by whatever means,
he also gains a certain power over other people
... What really endows the social organism with
potent and productive forces is the work which
individual skills and capacities perform with the
aid of capital. What harms the social organism, on
the other hand, is when people whose own skills
and abilities do not fit them to undertake such
work, nevertheless find themselves in the possession
of capital due to some circumstance or other.
They wield financial power. What does it actually
mean to have capital? It means that you can get a
number of people to work in accordance with your
intentions; that you have power over the work done
by a number of people.[8]

Nowadays, ownership of business enterprises comprises
two groups of rights:
1. Power to determine the company's work: owners (for
   instance, shareholders in a company) set the aims and
   dictate the company organisation, appoint the company
   managers and can also fire them.
2. Power to determine profit distribution, increase or
   reduction in capital and use of the results of a liquidation.

As threefolding sees it, company management and the use
of means of production are a matter for the entrepreneurs
themselves. To direct a company requires skills gained
through training and experience, and largely determines
hierarchical and collegial structures. This is applied cultural

life. This is probably one of the most important ideas in the threefold social organism, and endows capitalism, which is not simply dismissed, with a form in which its harmful aspects can be overcome.

> Only when all positions necessary in economic life are appointed and administered by the cultural sphere, when people with individual skills are integrated into economic life through this sphere, will we arrive at a healthy, fruitful social situation. For only by this means will we be able to separate ownership of private capital from administration of this capital in order to benefit the healthy social organism.[9]

This new view of ownership has consequences for the meaning of equity or net assets. Nowadays the latter indicate that a company belongs to its owners insofar as it is not burdened by external capital. If there is no one in a company who can describe it as his private property, equity loses this meaning, serving instead largely as reserve for planned and unforeseen expenses, and indicating whether a company is credit-worthy.

The net income of the enterprise (value creation) is primarily there to provide a livelihood for all co-workers who have contributed to the operating profit. For this reason the net income can be distributed according to principles and methods described in Chapter 2. Such changes in ownership or property law will be strongly resisted by financial powers that have acquired majority shareholdings and continue to acquire them.

5. Sustainability and the Polarity of Agriculture and Industry

5.1 Balancing resources

Economic growth should not continue as it is, since it is leading to the death of the earth and humanity. In 1972 the Club of Rome published texts to awaken general awareness of this. Twenty years later, in June 1992, 17,000 people met at the Rio Summit to discuss sustainable development. Governments from 178 countries and many non-governmental organisations were represented there. Twenty years later we cannot say that nothing has happened, but it is far too little. People stand by and wait for governments to enforce economic sustainability by legislative measures. Laws, however, are passed in the context of political conflict where opposing interests come powerfully into play.

The economy would be sustainable if we only used as many resources as would leave the same amount available for future generations. We are a long way from this; and it seems to me that we have no idea how to achieve such a thing. Consumption of resources is most injurious in countries rich in raw materials. The large amount of money that enters their economies falls into the hands of a few who buy weapons with it to consolidate their power or to wage civil wars. Between 1980 and 2010, Nigeria earned almost 250 billion dollars from oil exports, but its economy shrank, and Lagos is now a run-down city with high levels of criminality. Many countries rich in resources fail to achieve prosperity. In oil-rich Venezuela, two-thirds of the population live in poverty. Terms such as 'cursed with resources' and 'the paradox of wealth' have been coined to describe such situations. The American economist Joseph Stiglitz, one of the fiercest critics of globalisation, who held key appointments at the International Monetary Fund, the World Bank and in the Clinton administration, and today is a professor at Columbia University, New York, points out that resource-rich countries lose all basis for their livelihood once their resources have been plundered. He says that they should invest money in their future while they have it so they can survive by their economic output at a later date.[1]

If we speak of investment today, we think of the development of industry and service companies that bring wealth and prosperity to countries poor in resources. The successful emerging nations too, such as Brazil, India and China, invest in line with this formula. It is possible for individual countries to do this, but if we think of the earth as a whole, this does not make up for resource depletion. We have learned to distinguish between finite and renewable resources. The second reproduce themselves while for the first we have no other option but to be sparing with them and reclaim as many raw materials from waste products as we can. But finite resources will certainly diminish – some faster, others more slowly. How can a country compensate for these losses? This is only possible if there is a third category, which we can call *multipliable* resources. Globalisation experts don't speak of these; but they exist in areas of the economy which produce goods with the aid of living nature: in agriculture and forestry.

One in three people in the world live in poverty and destitution, and a billion people suffer from malnutrition, many of them in countries rich in resources but otherwise poor.

According to the UN's Food and Agricultural Organization, the earth would be able to feed the 12 billion people predicted for 2050. But this is surely only possible through sustainable, organic and ecological agriculture and forestry, rather than by the global spread of industrial, resource-consuming agriculture. In rich countries farmers have low status because of their small share in gross productivity; but in many poor countries, where they contribute a great deal to the gross product, they are exploited by industrialised nations that force them to produce coffee, cotton, tropical fruits, etc., and export these to wealthy lands. Agriculture can enable people to feed and clothe themselves, but it does not make them rich. Yet riches certainly are made by exploiting the agricultural work of others.

It is clear today that the place of agriculture within the economy is crucial for sustainability. We must therefore examine this in more detail and will then discover that, when scarcely anyone had thought of such a thing, Rudolf Steiner highlighted it in a way that appeared very exotic at the time, and has still hardly been understood by economic theorists.

5.2 How important is agriculture?

Whereas agriculture in Afghanistan accounts for 60 per cent of the gross national product, it only represents one per cent in Germany. The poor esteem accorded it in consequence, means, among other things, that more and more fertile land is being built on. In the small country of Switzerland, construction eats up a square metre of land every second, including a good deal of fertile arable land. In Germany it is 11.5 m^2 per second. During the world wars people in Europe were still worried about having enough to eat. A hint of this remains in Swiss legislation which requires sufficient available arable land for times of restricted imports, and so

440,000 hectares of prime arable land must be protected from construction. But as many municipalities have no detailed land-use maps, it is impossible to tell whether this protected area still exists.

It is well known that agriculture is the focus of grave problems in economics policy. In many developed industrial countries, it is only kept alive through subsidies. In international negotiations and agreements, agricultural economics takes up a disproportionate amount of time. Rather than agriculture itself causing these problems, it appears that the relationship between agriculture and industry, while not properly understood, is nevertheless exploited ruthlessly.

In the eighteenth-century economic theory of the physiocrats, agriculture was still accorded the highest status. At the time, 80 per cent of people lived and worked as farmers. Around 1890, after the first great Industrial Revolution, half of all people still worked in agriculture. At this time world trade was developing thanks to steamships. Grain for the whole world was traded on the Chicago stock exchange. In the 1870s a problem arose in relation to this because grain prices fell heavily on the world market, confronting European agriculture with a battle for survival. In Germany, in 1879, a protective tariff on grain was introduced in Germany to safeguard the country's agriculture. The British responded differently: they shifted their food supply to imports from overseas, sacrificing their own agriculture and transforming grain fields into large sheep pastures.

5.3 Price speculation with our daily bread

Because the price of grain kept on falling, Germany was forced to increase the protective tariff first threefold and then fivefold by 1887. To justify this it was said that the world was producing too much grain; that the fall in prices was due to foreign competition. These were problems that continue to play a role in the world agricultural market today. Bismarck was interested in examining these reasons more carefully, and commissioned Gustav Ruhland, an agrarian well known at the time, to travel the world and see what was going on in different locations. By the time Ruhland returned from his world trip in 1890, Bismarck had fallen from power. Ruhland later became a professor in Zurich and in Freiburg in Switzerland, and wrote a three-volume work on the system of political economy, which nowadays can only be found in specialist historical libraries. He had discovered during his travels that the prices on the world market had not fallen because of surpluses or cheaper competition: 'International agricultural competition did not turn out to be a production problem, since farmers in various parts of the globe were all suffering in roughly equal ways.'

Ruhland discovered a quite different reason for the problem. At the corn exchange in Chicago, people were engaged in forward or futures trading, as in today's bonds and currency speculation, and also in the grain market. A vendor and a purchaser agree a contract in the winter or spring for supply the following summer. Both try to estimate how prices will develop by the summer, and conclude a kind of bet with each other about this. They agree a price, determined at the time they sign the agreement. Come the summer, if the price is lower the vendor makes a profit because he can sell at a higher than market price; and the purchaser will make a corresponding loss. If the price is higher, the reverse is the case. No speculative futures trading can happen without price fluctuations (volatility), and this remains the principle underpinning the massive gains and losses in currency speculation and derivatives trading on stock markets. If there were no price fluctuations but instead fair trading with stable prices, speculation would wither away.

But prices can also be hugely affected by futures trading,

and this was already the case in grain speculation at the end of the nineteenth century. As a speculator nowadays I can offer a large quantity of grain for summer supply even if I do not have this grain. Of course I can plan to buy in this grain shortly before the supply date, in the hope it will then be cheaper than the price I have agreed today in the forward trading agreement. But having observed price fluctuations for a while, I can once again execute my grain sale as a futures agreement when the date draws near, so that I then have the grain in summer that I have to supply. If my first, completely unreal offer was large enough, I have been able to affect the market and make the price fall to my advantage. In currency futures trading, big business is done in this way, and has no real basis. It is said that only 2.5 per cent of 'futures' are actually performed. 97.5 per cent are closed out.

Ruhland discovered, at any rate, that the collapse of grain prices had been caused not by the real economy but by futures trading of this kind. A hundred years ago he believed that enduring truths were enshrined in the doctrines of the physiocrats, three of which I will reproduce here:[2]

◊ Mother Earth remains the sole source of wealth
◊ The prosperity of farmers is fundamental to the prosperity of a nation
◊ The state must intervene in the economy to ensure that an average grain price is established, which is acceptable to both producers and consumers.

We may view these ideas sympathetically; however they are only partial truths that do not accord with reality. We need further ideas and perspectives.

5.4 'The greatest problem we face today'

In 1919, when Rudolf Steiner embarked on his wide-ranging plan for a new social order in Germany and Switzerland, he noted the very greatest contrast between agriculture and the rest of the economy. During a question-and-answer session in 1919, he spoke of the cause of the social problem, and responded to the question as to why a proletariat exists. Today we still have more or less the same issue in the ever-widening gulf between wealth and poverty, in unemployment, the struggle of the working poor and the gap between rich and poor nations. Steiner said that the cause of these discrepancies lay in the 'greatest problem we face today,' which has arisen with the coming of industrialism. And then he spoke the following astonishing sentences.

[The problem] is embodied in the fact that
all industrialism in the economy works with
a liability – this, and nothing else, is the case.
All industrialism, insofar as it keeps developing
continually through its means of production, works
in relation to the economy as a whole with negative
equity.

How is this negative equity covered?
It is covered solely by land ... solely by what the
land produces ... All problems relating to wages,
capital and prices in modern life originate in the
fact that the surplus created by land production
migrates to meet the negative equity in industry.[3]

To understand these comments we will have to examine them word by word. Steiner does not say 'industry' but 'all industrialism' works with a negative equity, and we must include here also tractors, threshing machines and milking machines.[4] And what is meant here by negative equity? Does industry make a loss? That cannot be the meaning, for it was not the case at the time. Steiner says that industrialism is working with a *liability*, thus he is speaking not of the profit and loss account but of the balance sheet.

He expressly refers also to the means of production whereby industrialism keeps developing. When a means of production is used, and is recorded as an asset in the balance sheet, it is written down in value year by year because it gradually depreciates; or, in Steiner's proposal, it is immediately written off because it should no longer be sold as a commodity. Even if their value is written off the moment they are procured, machines and equipment still have a value that depreciates year on year. This is their productivity value and not an asset value with a sale price. In Steiner's formulation he is concerned only with the asset side of the balance sheet, and in the overall economy he compares industrialism's asset side with that of land production. The productivity of a company comes to expression in its assets. The productivity reliant on premises and machinery gradually declines and must repeatedly be renewed through new investments. By contrast, the productivity of agricultural and forested land, with all its natural foundations, its plants and animals, does not decline in value but can in fact increase with good cultivation practices. A tractor which I buy today comes to an end of its useful life after, say, thirty years, and is then no longer there. A horse or a cow can produce a whole herd in the same period if the necessary pastureland is available.

Since the nineteenth century, universities and training colleges have taught that agriculture is a business like any other, and that its aim is to make a profit. After long resistance to this idea, farmers eventually accepted it in the past sixty years. Large swathes of agriculture have a commercial orientation, involving high input of mineral fertilisers, fodder and toxic substances, leading to ecological damage and waste that has to be disposed of or recycled in ways that do as little damage as possible to the environment. Organic agriculture – the only form that can be seen as truly sustainable – cultivates living processes without feeds and fertilisers brought from outside the farm. However, it does use the support of machines and energy, and in this is no different from industry. Its organic 'waste products' (dung, harvest left-overs) do not impair the environment but enhance the soil's life and the health and productivity of agriculture. Here agriculture is engaged in *primary production*, whereas industry involves *refining production*. Organic agriculture makes our natural foundations (soil fertility) healthier, whereas industry depletes them and reduces their value.

As primary production, land production is the foundation of all economic activity, and is therefore certainly not despised by the great economic powers. Rather, they make strenuous efforts to take possession of as much land as possible along with the greatest possible proportion of agrarian output. A great deal of money can be made from seed, fertiliser and pesticides on the one hand, and from processing agricultural produce and trading on the other. Land production itself is weakened by misguided forms of social organisation, so that it has to be sustained by subsidies in wealthy nations.

5.5 Primary production without replacement nutrients

What has been so far outlined is not yet sufficient for a clear perception of the nature of land as means of production, and the difference between agriculture and industry. This is only possible if we draw on Rudolf Steiner's Agricultural Course, given to farmers in Silesia in 1924. Something quite new was added to the picture there. Steiner showed that it is possible to produce something in agriculture and pass on or sell this produce without having to return corresponding quantities of substance to the soil again. Mainstream scientists still consider this impossible. Their theories state that without using replacement nutrient substitutes, the soil will be depleted. But in many organic farms, practical experience has shown something different. There, thanks to careful soil husbandry using manure, crop planting and animal husbandry, such depletion has not occurred but soil fertility and soil health have been enduringly improved.

In the Agriculture Course Steiner says that a 'progressive process' arises through a closed circulation of substances between the land, plants serving as fodder and animal manure, which adapt to each other in an increasingly harmonious way. From year to year, he says, the farm will improve if as few substances as possible are brought in from outside in the form of fertiliser or fodder. Certainly one would have to monitor in every individual instance how far it is possible to do this at any time. But the aim of agricultural management, according to Steiner, is to create this closed circulation of substances in relation to fodder and manuring. Year by year this will lead to the farm increasingly becoming a better, more self-contained farm 'individuality'.

5.6 Organism and individuality

We speak of the human individual. What do we mean by this? The human being is not just an organism like a plant or an animal. A natural organism has processes it can keep functioning for a whole lifetime, and even pass these on to offspring. When an animal is born, within a very short time it has all the capacities it needs for its life. We human beings on the other hand arrive helplessly in the world and have to learn a lot of things by effort, not just when we're young but through into old age. But we have a capacity that animals do not: we can be creative and develop new insights and knowledge.

This creative autonomy of the human being is a quality that distinguishes the individual from a mere organism. According to Steiner this also applies to the 'farm individuality'. This does not just mean that farmers should be creative in their work but that nature itself can produce something new in the agricultural setting. Here higher spiritual forces are at work, not only the vital forces that act in every organism. These higher forces lead to health in field and stable, and to higher productivity.

The new element that enters earthly nature through agriculture originates in a spiritual realm. In agriculture today there is a distinct need to increasingly understand the nature of this spiritual element, in small, laborious steps. Spirit exists in everything earthly and material. But if we look out into the cosmos we find ever-diminishing matter there and ever-increasing spirit. Steiner spoke in the Agriculture Course a great deal about the stars and planets because they consist to a small degree only of physical matter and are above all spiritual in nature and work down spiritually upon the physical earth. For this reason too he said that agriculture involves drawing in cosmic – that is spiritual – forces and substances with the aid of silica, and anchoring them in earthly processes through the carbon cycle and humus formation. If this is successful, no depletion or deficiencies will occur. In biodynamics, much of the work aims to open the soil, as well as plants and animals, to these cosmic influences.[5]

This new beginning in agriculture in 1924 made the contrasts between agriculture and industry a great deal more apparent. We can summarise them roughly as follows:

Agriculture	Industry
1. Primary production	Refining production
2. Living whole	Division of labour and collaboration
3. Renewal of resources	Waste creation
4. Attentiveness to nature	Distance from natural world through to indifference
5. Personal connection, love for specifics	Anonymity, universal human love
6. Personal interest	Quality assurance through external checks
7. Small-scale structures and self-sufficiency	World trade

1. Agriculture creates something new and thus is engaged in primary production, whereas industry produces valuable goods by transforming raw materials and intermediate goods into useful things.

2. Agriculture is productive where it is cultivated holistically. The soil becomes more fertile through humus formation and manuring, and creates new potential. In industry, by contrast, higher productivity is usually achieved by a division of labour. A finished product only arises through collaboration. Intelligent division of labour involves collaboration as a fundamental principle of the modern industrial economy, making work more productive. At the same time this makes time available for spiritual and cultural activities.

3. Agriculture renews and improves resources: air, water and soil with the varieties of plants and species of animals upon the land. Industry consumes resources and produces waste which has to be recycled and reintegrated into the natural world in as environmentally-friendly a

way as possible. This is never completely successful however.

4. In his work the farmer must dedicate the greatest attention to nature and its produce. Industrial workers, due to the division of labour, have less and less to do directly with the products. They stand or sit at machines which are programmed to run by themselves.

5. Through division of labour work becomes anonymous. I do not know who made the steering wheel of my car, and the person who made it does not know me. If people found it possible to work for other reasons than just a wage, the industrial worker's only motive would be to work because they know what they do is needed by others whom they do not know. Rudolf Steiner called this 'universal human love' as stimulus for labour. This does not arise by itself but it can be cultivated if general education enables us to perceive the value of all people as spiritual-physical beings. On the other hand, anyone who works in agriculture has a different point of departure. They first have to fully connect with the work they are doing. Steiner placed great importance on the farmer's personal connection with manure and all living things in the farm organism. This is not a return to the old-fashioned love of a craftsman for what he has made. Agriculture requires a substantially enhanced love for the work and an increased sense of personal connection with the living creatures the farmer cares for. Over long eras, agriculture and manual crafts had this love of their work in common. Insofar as division of labour in industry has brought about development in one direction, a counterweight must be created in the other, where farmers consciously cultivate their personal connection with the farm and their work in a new way, as the precondition of productivity. If they look beyond the boundaries of their farm, they know they are working for the benefit of the whole earth and the

progress of humanity. Thus they arrive at universal human love too, by another route.

6. Steiner pointed out that the division of labour and capitalism – the latter necessary for the former to provide the means of production – bring with them a risk of declining quality. For this reason industry has to give ever keener attention to quality assurance. This is necessary in agriculture too, partly in similar ways to industry, but in important respects also different because it involves personal connections and relationships between producers and consumers.

7. Agriculture is always in danger when producing mass goods for the market and raw materials for industrial refining. If it does so it is exposed to strongly competitive forces since industry is indifferent to which farmer supplies these mass goods. If sales are uncertain (or are made so) farmers try to undercut each other's prices to get rid of their goods. This disadvantage can only be reduced through direct marketing and small-scale and therefore easily surveyed markets. Agriculture thrives best where direct, small-scale trading structures prevail. Every nation and region ought primarily to feed itself from its own land. In exporting countries, only land not needed for producing food for local inhabitants should be used to grow export crops such as coffee, cotton, tropical fruit, etc. There is great awareness of this now in welfare groups concerned with poor countries.

5.7 Competition and self-sufficiency

Market economy theory makes it harder to understand these things. The theory states that in competitive markets not only are prices created through supply and demand but that the reverse is also true: that supply and demand are regulated by price changes. In Section 2.10. we showed that this is not a generally reliable reversal. There are differences between types of commodity. Theorists like to demonstrate market laws by citing goods that we don't absolutely need, such as ice-cream. The more an ice-cream costs the less people buy it, and the less therefore is produced. The markets for such goods is elastic depending on price. In agriculture and the basic food market by contrast, supply (production) and demand (consumption) scarcely adapt to price levels and are not very elastic relative to price. However expensive it becomes to buy food, we will have to buy it if we are not to starve. If food becomes very cheap we may perhaps treat ourselves to tastier meals, but overall we will not buy more than fills us. On the other hand, it has repeatedly been found that falling prices do not reduce production supply but force farmers to increase it so that they can go on earning their livelihood. In general this harms nature, which is depleted and damaged further even if the number of farms declines over long periods. The pressure on nature can only be reduced if farmers are relieved of price pressures.

These laws are a major reason why the governments of rich countries regulate agricultural markets by price-support measures so that they are no longer free markets, or directly support farmers through income subsidies. The only purely economic alternative involves market participants applying the principle of self-sufficiency as far as possible, either by buying directly from farmers or insisting that the origin of produce is exactly specified so that they know where their food has been grown. An extreme form of self-sufficiency, CSA (Community Supported Agriculture) was described in Section 3.2.

In agriculture, despite the division of labour that is far advanced here too, self-sufficiency is still regarded as a valid principle. To understand this, we can assume that everyone has an entitlement to land on which they can walk, work and sleep and where their food grows. Today our right to land is made impossible by the way in which land ownership is managed. The right to eat, on the other hand, is internationally acknowledged. The UN established a post of Special Rapporteur for this purpose, which was held by Jean Ziegler from 2000 to 2008. He tried to make headway against the shameless machinations of global corporations and governments in poor countries. The right to land necessary for procuring food applies even for those who do not undertake agricultural labour themselves. At the same time, all people retain the right to grow their own food. The division of labour has gradually led people to distance themselves from agriculture. The smith makes ploughs, axes, saws and knives and in return receives his food. The basket-weaver can cut his own willow rods and still works in close proximity to agriculture. The smith needs iron as his raw material, and cannot supply this himself. As division of labour increases, an industrial economy removes itself from agriculture. But as consumers, people ought not to distance themselves in the same way from their region's agriculture. Yet they do so if they buy up foodstuffs on an anonymous market which they leave to the blind workings of supply and demand.

In the industrial economy local self-provision or self-sufficiency is disadvantageous since it makes goods more expensive, whereas the division of labour makes them cheaper. This is also true in agriculture to begin with. But here it is easy to see that food declines in quality the further we remove ourselves from self-provision. It becomes cheap, but too expensive in environmental and health terms; and it therefore puts up the cost of medical care so that overall a loss is incurred. One can ruin whole nations by removing their capacity to provide regionally for themselves. It is true nevertheless that at times of poor harvests different economic regions can help each other thanks to global trading. In industry too, division of labour brings about a decline in quality, but here it is less damaging and can be kept within bounds by quality assurance. The latter however can do nothing to remedy decline in denatured, industrialised farming. Self-sufficiency in agriculture means working not only for gain but for the continuance of the earth and humanity.

The close connection between people and the locality where their food grows is made more difficult nowadays because of their desire to live together in big cities. In many countries they are forced to do so. This tendency is increasing hugely at present and is one of the greatest problems of our times. People migrate to the cities among other things because they hope to find work there. The modern economy's centralistic tendencies also have a dire effect on population distribution. Decentralisation is one of the chief concerns of the economic reform movement. Many businesses, including industrial ones, could easily be sited in villages. Art too thrives in decentralised locations as well as or better than in cities. Concerts and plays can be performed perfectly well in regional localities. Rudolf Steiner held the view that city economies make the market unclear:

> Associative economics would mean, above all, that a whole number of factories move from the city to the country ... If the market is there, with villages around it, even if it adheres to the principle of supply and demand it will be far less damaging in economic terms – as long as there are no crooks involved – than if a city economy arrives. The latter radically alters the whole relationship between producers and consumers. Then we no longer have villages which regulate their market themselves, but instead we open up everything to all kinds of possibilities that exist when the producer-consumer relationship is no longer clear, when it gets muddled. And this is the case when people live together in cities.

Centralisation of the economy in cities would be overcome through proper social threefolding:

> Over longer periods, but actually not all that long, it would become apparent that civil servants, central colleges and so forth would mainly be in the cities – in other words, the cultural sphere and the rights sphere – whereas economic life and the rights life belonging to it would be decentralised.[6]

Alongside agriculture and industry we ought to speak also of the caring professions and of inventors, consultants and organisational experts, as well as the fields of education and research. These areas have a very wide scope today, and they too are distinct from industry. In this chapter we restricted ourselves to areas of the economy that produce goods and commodities from material things, that is, agriculture and industry; and these represent two opposite poles of a whole. If we take modern biodynamic agriculture as a model we can definitely say that agriculture and industry must in various respects balance out each other's one-sided tendencies. This can better be done in villages than in large cities.

5.8 Associations between industry and agriculture

As we have already seen, Rudolf Steiner proposed developing a network organisation that would itself fulfil the social tasks and duties which today are foisted on the state. This was to be a non-centralised organisational form. People and businesses that have economic ties with each other should voluntarily begin to form joint organisations as a natural consequence of the collaboration necessary in a modern economy based on the division of labour. Today's company mergers in the egotistic interests of capital profit are like a caricature of what is actually needed.

Steiner meant something different by these associations than a syndicate, union or cooperative. The people and companies connecting with each other should not just share the same business interests, but associations should comprise reciprocating counterparts, in other words those who wish to sell something and those who need it – producers with their respective purchasers and consumers. For agriculture, partners in this sense are all the people who need food. Most of these earn their incomes in other areas of the economy, and this income is dependent on the price of goods that they produce there. When we speak of prices it is never a matter of a single price in isolation but always of diverse commodity prices, which are in turn dependent on all the factors existing in the economy. The task of the associations is to observe these factors and recommend, introduce and facilitate corresponding measures. This is why competent people drawn from companies must gather together in the associations, and have the ability to implement the necessary measures. These do not involve fixing prices through market power, as cartels would do, but instead such things as changing or adjusting production to ensure that reasonable prices can arise in the markets.

While it is good if I pay a fair price when I buy bananas – this should ensure that farmers in the country of origin will benefit – but it is better if we conclude associative agreements to ensure that the farmers on their land can feed themselves and their families, along with their whole country, and only cultivate bananas for export on land they do not need for that primary purpose. The price of bananas on the market might then either be higher or lower than it is today. If we wish to judge whether it is right, we will need to relate it to the price of goods which the banana-producing country imports because it cannot produce them, or cannot do so as cheaply. The change to an economy in a banana-producing country described here must be introduced in that country itself. But in countries where we import bananas we must try to ensure that we do not impede this process or make it impossible, as we are currently doing through state subsidies to agriculture which are only possible in developed countries; and by the fact that we inveigle undeveloped countries into borrowing capital. This compels them to orientate their agriculture to export in order to be able to pay interest on their debt.

By properly integrating agriculture into the whole economy in this way, we achieve structures which will prevent global economic centralism from imposing itself; and this will be true also in industry, for in the latter case regionalisation can also make economic sense. What can be manufactured in Europe does not have to be shipped across the ocean from the Far East. It is also not necessary for European watches to 'conquer' the Chinese market. Nowadays production is transferred to low-wage countries where social conditions are dire and where less tax has to be paid. This is profitable in the short term for individual companies, primarily the owners of capital, but is uneconomic in the long term and socially objectionable. International corporations tend to think centralistically. They can more easily manipulate the global economy than is possible in a clearly manageable regional economy. Associations, on the other hand, are developed from regional grass roots on federalist principles.

If we consider all this, it is no longer so surprising that Steiner's proposal for the first necessary steps was the creation of associations between industry and agriculture, since here there is the greatest need for balancing measures. In such associations all those involved would have to have some understanding of the polarity between industry and agriculture, and thus also of primary production and fertility in the agricultural organism or individuality. It is not simply a matter of distinguishing industry and agriculture, since there are machines and buildings in agriculture too. Industrialism and capitalism encroach deeply on agriculture. Through their labour, farmers produce economically valuable produce from the soil and the whole of nature's living context, and by means of machines and buildings they make their labour efficient. They thus work with two different means of production: nature and technology; but these are opposite in their character. Thus the distinction drawn should be one between the productivity of the fertile soil, and the tools and equipment created by human beings. In lecture 13 of *World Economy*, Steiner showed that technical and organisational inventions save on manual work. This rationalisation has occurred in agriculture to a very great degree, and even in organic agriculture work with machines has greatly increased, with both advantages and disadvantages. Economic values originate in the cultivated soil on the one hand and in labour made more efficient on the other. Fertile soil can increase its productivity through the way it is used and cared for, but machines and buildings always decline in value through usage.

Such considerations provide us with the foundations for gradually gaining better understanding of the position of agriculture and forestry within the overall economy, so that we can start to solve the urgent problems of sustainability in the economy itself rather than in the political domain. If we consume the earth's resources and are unable to recover them from waste products, we have to know that we can only compensate for this loss by improving the vitality and productivity of fertile land. This is not a task for state policies but for the economy. The work of the Swiss company Remei with cotton growers in India and Tanzania can serve as a model for this. We need to enable farmers everywhere and in every region to undertake the kind of work necessary to ensure soil fertility – which is an immense task. This work will only thrive if farmers undertake it in a way they can understand, and with the insights they possess and can perhaps develop with our help. This is development aid which has to flourish individually everywhere, in every region.

6. The Endeavour of Social Threefolding

6.1 The importance of threefolding today

This book began with tangible social problems, and aims to show that the independent actions of only a few, rather than state-run politics, have made major contributions to solving them. It hopes to stimulate further such practical actions, and points here to the following especially important innovations:

1. Monetary administration in the economic sphere,
2. The separation of labour and income in every company and in the economic collaboration between companies,
3. The administration of land and productive capital by the cultural sphere.

Of these innovations, two relate to economic organisation and one to that of the cultural sphere. These two domains are fundamentally distinct from the rights sphere or rights state. We have already seen that it is not easy to fully conceive the very different organisational forms that arise in the economy and cultural life, out of the intrinsic nature of these domains. State administration is tasked with safeguarding and enforcing law that applies generally to all citizens. However, it is not identical with the whole domain of rights and law, since the economy and cultural life also create legal structures for their organisms, doing so through contractual agreements. These distinctions between three different administrative structures give rise to many practical consequences; and the more these come into being, the more clearly does the complex threefold nature of all society become apparent.

Rudolf Steiner first described the concept of the threefold social order in detail in 1919, not as a theory but as a call to action, both in practical ways and in one's thinking. The previous chapters have repeatedly shown how relevant Steiner's proposals are still – never more so than today. This needs to be said to all those who think that Steiner's ideas need to be adapted to current social realities after ninety years, and that much has to be seen differently now. The enquiries on which the previous chapters are based have on the contrary shown that Steiner's ideas, considered from a practical standpoint, enable us to gain insight into the deeper context of modern society and its workings, and reveal potential solutions that are scarcely thought of today because they remain largely unknown.

6.2 An individual's autonomy

The key idea of threefolding is freedom. In the social order, the state is not the highest and ultimate authority from which all proceeds and which has the last word in everything. This principle of sovereignty which has been regarded as a characteristic of the state since the advent of absolutism, was initially attributed to the monarch and in those days directly derived from divine right. Since the French Revolution, we speak of national sovereignty realised through a democratic form of government. In both cases, the sovereign state is conceived as the summit of all society. This model of human society is one our thinking feels very comfortable with. We build every machine with a central steering or control system. It is easy for us to think in terms of centralised systems.

The separation of powers, which every child learns about today in lessons on history and citizenship, was a great step towards limiting state centralism. It arose from a desire for freedom and contradicts the simple logic of sovereignty. One of its prime aspects is the independence of the courts. In practice however, political parties have a decisive influence on the choice of judges, as they do on all state decisions. Judges are appointed by the state body which is regarded as supreme, whether this be the elected parliament or the president. The division of power is thus subordinate to state sovereignty and has therefore not fully achieved its goal.

Nowadays the principle of freedom requires a further, more comprehensive step. This not only involves state organisation but the whole of the social order. The state intervenes in ever more detailed ways in public life, and laws are becoming more wide-ranging and complex. Contemporary needs require the very opposite of this. People active and involved in different areas can themselves largely regulate their own affairs and concerns. This applies above all to educational, cultural and economic matters.

As modern people we refuse to be a cog in a large machine. Threefolding breaks out of this centralism, seeing the state as only one of three autonomous systems, none of which are predominant over the others. In each system people are sovereign in different ways: in the state through democratic decisions, in the economy through contractually agreed collaboration and in the cultural sphere through free acknowledgment of individual initiatives. Such a system is inconceivable as a mechanism; the parts of it would fall asunder and not form a whole. In living systems, however, relative autonomy of different parts is the rule, since the formative powers of the whole are at work in every part, and therefore every aspect is integrated into the whole through its inherent properties. Every individual is the bearer of these inner properties or qualities in the social realm. Each person is the highest entity or authority in the overall social organism.[1] This is why threefolding starts with the individual human being and not with the old sovereignty of the state. It depends on each individual's initiative whether threefolding comes into effect in social structures.

Rudolf Steiner's own actions seem to contradict this assertion. During the First World War he tried to persuade the monarchy governments of the two Central powers that threefolding was the only sensible goal of peace negotiations. Before the whole aristocratic regime departed from office, the nobility could have imposed threefolding from above, although its actual realisation would, even then, have had to proceed from below upwards. This was similarly apparent when, after the war, Steiner presented the threefold idea to the wider public, giving an impression that he wished to introduce it by political means. We surely misunderstand him if we assume this. His stance towards the work council movement in Germany was exemplary. He endorsed the spontaneous founding of staff associations or work councils in individual enterprises prior to any state legislation determining from above their form and function. Social structure has to arise from the interplay of the people who are themselves involved in it. In 1919 Steiner gave numerous lectures in factories in Stuttgart. It was always his concern to teach people to act out of their own insights.[2] In relation to threefolding he stressed on many occasions that it could only be achieved with those who understand it:

> In *Towards Social Renewal* I showed that this threefold social order can be initiated anywhere and everywhere as long as one seeks to do so, and really understands its purpose and meaning.[3]

> Only with the emergence of an increasing number of people, who have the honest will and courage first to understand this threefold idea in its radical

terms and then also to realise it, will what is needed for the well-being and emancipation of human beings come about in some way or other. This can be done wherever one stands, from any position in life – enough people with new ideas need to replace those with outmoded, unfruitful ideas.[4]

For anyone who is not a pessimist, there is only this way of thinking: how can we find enough people, as many as possible, who understand this threefold idea; for then we could actually realise it very quickly. I have never said this could be done in ten years' time. No, it could be done today at any and every point.[5]

The government's contribution to threefolding is not to introduce it, but only to permit it, and not to prevent free initiatives. The more we take socio-economic tasks and education into our own hands, the more the state can withdraw from the responsibilities it currently has.[6] There is only one domain from which the state should not withdraw. It must safeguard the rule of law, and this is its intrinsic task. The core areas of the state's jurisdiction are therefore the police and army, order and safety of traffic, safety and accident prevention, the fire service, prevention of harm to life or limb, protection of private property and anything that falls under laws applicable equally to all human beings.

In view of the situation today, some of the statements made here may well seem Utopian and impracticable. But this can change if, as has been attempted in this book, we try to form a clear picture of autonomous administration in the economy and in the cultural sphere and, as Steiner urged, we come to 'understand this threefold idea'.

6.3 Freedom and co-determination

The three ideals of the French Revolution, Liberty, Equality and Fraternity, have a dual relationship to freedom. On the one hand they are predicated on it as their foundation. If it were not possible for human beings to become free, equality and fraternity would not be possible either. Rudolf Steiner based his *Philosophy of Freedom*[7] on the *potential* autonomy of every individual, and this is the focus in all his works. At the same time, the ideals of equality and fraternity serve freedom, each in their own way, because they allow every individual to be a co-determining partner in society. In the democratic life of rights all responsible people have an equal entitlement to play their part. Economic matters are regulated by those involved in them and affected by them. They conclude agreements with each other, often involving mutual compromises. In the cultural-spiritual sphere, co-determination can only mean that we voluntarily acknowledge the free initiatives of individuals.

Rudolf Steiner himself said the following about the relationship between the *Philosophy of Freedom* and the threefold social order:

> We must continually focus on the way in which we live in social community. In fact, my book *Towards Social Renewal* is in a sense an enlargement of, or complementary to, my *Philosophy of Freedom*. The *Philosophy of Freedom* enquires into how an individual's powers can become free, and similarly *Towards Social Renewal* looks at what is necessary if a social organism is to be shaped in a way that enables individuals to develop freely. Basically, these are the two great questions that must preoccupy us today in public life.[8]

6.4 Do people first have to acquire social skills?

If it is true that everything depends on every human individual, then it seems obvious to suggest that every person should, first and foremost, acquire social skills and abilities. However, Rudolf Steiner showed that this is not the case.[9] It is normal for us to be antisocial in this day and age. Steiner even suggested that egotism, a necessary concomitant of modern, developing consciousness, will continue to increase as we continue to evolve into self-aware individuals. To create a counterbalance to this increase of antisocial forces, it is necessary to establish external social structures that gradually facilitate the growth of socialisation. This will not eradicate the antisocial forces in us, but cultivate social forces alongside them at the same time, so that these balance each other.

There are numerous social structures today which accentuate egotism and render social conduct more or less impossible. This is especially apparent in our wage system, which fundamentally appeals to egotism. This is why wage conflicts are regarded as normal, and unions as a necessary institution to undertake these battles. But in place of our wage system we could create institutions that continually prompt us not just to think of ourselves. These will not simply abolish our egotism but will give us opportunities to work at it and develop social forces.

Egotism is unleashed most strongly where economic interests clash with one another in the political domain, leading to power battles between political parties. Parties were created to fight out these conflicts of interest; and for this reason threefolding places importance on interests being dealt with in the economy and not in the political state. In the economy, forms of organisation must be developed which counteract egotism and continually urge us not only to perceive our own interests but also those of people with whom we have some connection. People's interest in each other is something Steiner describes as a first step towards developing social capacities.[10]

6.5 'I'm speaking of social impulses!'

Initially the threefold social organism appears to be a thought construct. But further study shows these ideas to be alive, capable of changing, adapting to reality and growing in the same way as living entities or creatures. This is why 'threefolding' does not offer new ideas but *impulses*. This word was an important one for Rudolf Steiner:

> It is not a superficial matter that an attempt has been made, based also on anthroposophy, to develop not social ideas, but social impulses. I still recall a time when there was much discussion of these things. I always felt obliged to say, 'I'm speaking of social impulses!' This really annoyed people, for naturally they thought I should have spoken of social *ideas*, since they could only conceive of ideas on the subject. The fact that I was speaking of impulses greatly irritated them. They could not see that I was offering impulses in order to invoke realities rather than abstract ideas. But naturally one has to express oneself first in abstract ideas.[11]

Over the past ninety years, the impulses of threefolding have given proof of their practical fruitfulness in small-scale projects. At the same time attempts have also been made to understand the construct of ideas around it and to extend this, and much valuable work has been done here too. So far, however, there are astonishingly many theoretical controversies on the subject. Why is this so?

6.6 Threefolding, not division into three

No one doubts that we can distinguish between the domains of rights life, the economy, and cultural life. They do not need to be *separated* from each other but instead *connected* with each other in the *right way*. It is precisely this that is meant by the 'threefolding of the social organism'. Today we face the challenge of organising each of the three spheres in a way that enables people to develop autonomy and responsibility and come fully into their own. In his course on *World Economics*, Steiner said in 1922:

> I have always objected to the phrase 'tripartition' or 'division into three'. It is like this: we have three elements or domains which exist already. How should we relate them to one another in a natural way so that they can work upon each other accordingly? The cultural-spiritual organism will largely be oriented to freedom. But economic life will naturally work into the spiritual organism, for otherwise professors would not get anything to eat. This will happen in precisely the right way if it proceeds from a different sphere; and therefore we need to develop an economic organism in a particular direction, a cultural organism in a different direction; and then also the state or legal organism. Only those who conceive of this threefold organism as a separation into three parts, a tripartition, object to this idea. And you will know of course that many have done so. I discovered that an interpreter of the idea gave lectures on the 'three parliaments' in the social organism. If you picture it like this, you're conceiving something impossible, since a parliament only exists in the state not in the free cultural and spiritual life. In that domain there can

only be a single individual who creates a sphere of
self-evident authority. In the economic realm there
can only be associations between people ...[12]

The threefold social organism is a whole which we cannot
comprehend with concepts we have developed in relation
to machines. Our concepts must become mobile enough to
depict living realities. Here some of the strongest resistance
arises to what is meant by threefolding. In our analytic and
abstract thought we like to see things nicely distinct and
separate so that we can observe them in a static state. But
this approach will never allow us to comprehend a living
interplay, which is only possible through patient, repeated
consideration and experience of living processes.[13] Rudolf
Steiner himself first derived the threefold social organism
from the human organism, examining the interplay between
psychological and physical, bodily processes.[14]

Thus social community between people is likewise
something alive that emerges and fades – an 'organism' in
fact. This can most clearly be seen in economic processes
where an individual is never able to elaborate a valid
judgment that applies universally. Only in the dialogue
between people of diverging interests in specific interaction
with each other can a useful evaluation come about. In the
economy, therefore, the first and most important challenge
is to organise such dialogue. Rudolf Steiner applied the
term 'associations' – a word that was current in his day –
to this mode of organisation.[15] One cannot theoretically
determine in advance how dialogue will unfold in such
associations but in each case one has to await what actually
happens.

Administration of the spiritual sphere is based on different
basic premises again, and is thoroughly individualistic.
Steiner-Waldorf Schools choose their own teachers. In
actively running the school it becomes apparent whether

they find acknowledgment for their work, and whether parents wish to entrust their children to them. The parents too are autonomous in their choice of school. Whether or not a school succeeds depends on how well teachers and parents work together.

7. The Further Development of Democracy

7.1 Two concepts in a single word

Democracy, a universally acclaimed value, is today regarded as safeguarding not only the popular vote and majority decisions but also as protecting minorities, human rights, freedom of education and research, freedom of entrepreneurial initiatives, free self-development, personal responsibility as opposed to paternalism, the willingness to compromise, social welfare and much else. We therefore throw into the pot of this concept a whole bunch of ingredients that we consider make life worth living in a modern society. But the democratic state cannot meet all these fundamental needs and fulfil these ideals unaided. As an undifferentiated, centralised system, democracy has risks and deficiencies which we encountered in previous chapters. We can easily picture centralised systems but, whether acting on a large or small scale, they lead to unfreedom. Threefolding makes greater demands on our imaginative capacities and thinking because it leaves much open in the economy and in cultural life, awaiting what will emerge from communities and dialogue. This openness and unpredictability, however, is an important aspect of the democratic ideal.

We not only use the term democracy in a comprehensive sense, however, but also to refer in a more limited way to democratic decisions based on voting which we become accustomed to from our youth. A school class discusses a class outing planned for the last week of term: some want to go on a bicycle trip while others would rather swim and go for a boat trip. Voices quickly call out, 'Let's vote on it!' That is easy – no further thoughts or discussions are needed, and each person sticks to what they first thought of. If everyone wants to do it this way, it can of course be done, but the resulting majority decision should not in itself be called a just and 'democratic' mode.

We can discern this best by citing some extreme examples. In the past, parliaments or referenda (in Switzerland) often voted on whether nuclear power stations should be built or not, and the results were often a very close call. If 51 or 52 per cent of voters were in favour of atomic energy, they compelled the other 48 or 49 per cent to live with a risk which these latter rejected. If risks and dangers are involved, it becomes particularly apparent that majority decisions are unjust and lead to a rule of the majority over a minority. Votes that result in a narrow majority turn democracy into a power struggle that cannot be differentiated from other forms of dominion emerging from power struggles. In a referendum the aim is to convince and cajole as many voting citizens as possible, using the arts of persuasion we call advertising or propaganda. If such advertising does not limit itself to information that leaves recipients free, it becomes associated with lies and deception. One party wishes to impose its view on the other, and rides roughshod over people's individual responsibility.

We will not get beyond this until we manage economic interests separately from the realm of politics and the state. General rules and principles of community life are only free of unjust, external rule if the rights life of the state is emancipated from all vested interests and applies only to the rules which are equal for all. Such rules are ones that every responsible person with an ordinary general level of education can evaluate. Let us take a simple example: every law student learns the phrase *Pacta sunt servanda* – agreements must be kept. No one questions this principle, whether it is enshrined in law or not. In the same way, many rules in civil law are self-evident and do not need to be reintroduced through the civil code. Legislators have formulated what was already generally accepted practice, the state thus enforcing its legal status.

A basic motif of democracy identifies all citizens with the state. Why then do so many citizens feel alienated from it? The democratic election of parliament has led to the creation of parties. Depending on the voting system (majority vote, proportional representation or another), there will be two or more parties who battle for power. The parties represent group interests of an economic, denominational or cultural kind, etc. The parliamentary or congressional lobby has great influence in representing certain interests to its members. Only if the state is increasingly relieved of economic and cultural responsibilities can it start to focus on things which affect all citizens equally, without vested interests. Then power in the state will be used to ensure that all people have an equal entitlement. State administration, with its compulsory measures, exists to defend the law and not to determine its content. Thus the state can once again become a concern of all citizens.

7.2 Further development of the law

In the law as it stands there are three procedures which allow it to be developed further. The first involves the legislative power of the state enacting new laws. These are first discussed in parliament or congress and then decided by majority decision. On the one hand MPs or congressmen are governed by their own insights but on the other also by the interests they must represent as party members. In modern democratic countries it is also often stated that 'the law' says this or that. In absolutist monarchies this was a legitimate form of expression since the law-giver was a person. This was still true in the Renaissance and was expressly described by Machiavelli. Frederick the Great of Prussia in the book *Anti-Machiavelli* which he wrote while Crown Prince, described himself as the first servant of the state. By this he meant that the power of rulership was accorded to the abstract notion of the state and that the king was only this state's representative.

Nowadays we understand the state as a very abstract form of rule that is not invested in natural persons such as monarchs. The state became a legal person, and so we believe that we can say 'the state does this or that'. However, in democracy the concept of legislature only describes a procedure, and today therefore it is imprecise and rather misleading to say that 'legislators' decide what should become law. We ought instead to say that in the democratic process *we* decide what is to be the law. State laws tell us that such and such *ought* to be the case, and thus acquire the form of a command which we should obey. But as responsible individuals we would prefer to guide development in a direction where we can say, 'This is what we *wish*.'[1]

The second procedure is part of the task of judges who in each new actual case interpret positive (human-made) law – which means existing laws, court decisions, common law and legal custom – and apply it to the specific case. Every time they do so they also alter and broaden the law as a whole, which never acquires a complete or final form. Enacting justice in each case is a task of the cultural sphere. As we mentioned in the third part of Section 2.9, Rudolf Steiner assigned judges in criminal and civil law proceedings to the cultural sphere, saying they ought not to be organs of the state nor determined or chosen by the latter. State administration should only, and only where necessary, implement the law ascertained by judges. Every court decision develops the law further to a lesser or greater degree.[2]

The third procedure is to be found in private or civil law. Through agreements and statutes that observe current law we can shape our civil law relationships ourselves.

If we only think of state or political legislature when envisaging the law's development, we forget the other processes also vital for democracy. Law does not begin with state legislation since new legal measures can only be declared binding for all once a general view of the law has already been established, and a majority approves it in parliament or referenda. In a true 'rights state', a decision will only arise if the overwhelming majority of the people agree or abstain, thus declaring their willingness to stand behind the decision. We described this form of decision-making in Section 2.9. In civil law, in fact, unanimity is the general precondition for agreements and suchlike being accepted. The rights state can also be further developed in this direction. Democracy cannot mean that the nation rules *over* itself. Rulership within the state is only necessary where right must be defended against wrong, and for this purpose state administration is equipped with police and military powers. It applies physical enforcement such as fines and arrests not as retribution but in order to assure public safety and security.

In the modern state, justice is enshrined in laws. Emperor Justinian undertook the first comprehensive codification of laws in the sixth century, ordaining that all of Roman law, as it had developed through many centuries, should be recorded in the *Corpus Iuris Civilis*. Justice formulated as law stands above the human being: all can invoke it and must obey it, and the state with its administrative apparatus ensures that they do. In relation to justice understood in this way, people cannot feel themselves to be *intrinsically human* but only *citizens of the state*. In Roman times this was a positive achievement since it guided people, insofar as they were citizens, towards legal equality. In the course of Roman history, however, the idea of the state and of state power, became increasingly paramount. This late, authoritarian form of Roman law survived in the Roman Catholic Church, and in the Middle Ages was also increasingly adopted by worldly rulers since they wished to govern through a centralised bureaucracy. In Napoleon's military dictatorship, codification of law reached a new high point in 1804 with the *Code Civile* or *Code Napoléon*, the model for modern civil codes. In the course of all these developments, the state increasingly distanced itself from human beings, so that many came to regard it as something alien.

The written form of legislation is of great importance because it creates clarity and contributes to the law's stability. New legal regulations should not, however, be created simply in writing but must reflect our prevailing sense of justice. We can all know what is right or wrong through our innate sense of justice. This fact alone gives law its validity and creates the greatest possible legal stability. Written legislation and judicial verdicts aim to serve justice by applying this moral feeling and raising it into awareness.[3]

Applying one's sense of justice in legal proceedings is founded on life experience and much detailed knowledge of the law, as well as precise insight into an individual case. It is not a matter of mere feeling judgments but of carefully considered ones, based on the idea that every human being is a whole spiritual being, however different each person's gifts and impediments are. This is why the figure of Justice is portrayed with a pair of scales and a blindfold. Every case should be weighed up in a completely non-partisan way so that the verdict is generally applicable. But Justice also has a sword, because justice must be implemented in a way that prevents 'might' being 'right'. Pacifism leads only to a situation where the most violent or powerful can hold sway.

There are many people who only wish to behave well or reasonably if everyone else does, because the law demands it of everyone. It is right to think in this way as regards existing laws. But we should be careful not to demand something new of all citizens via new state legislation and regulations. The state ought not to create new laws to determine what is good or bad conduct by citizens, since this is something that responsible people themselves determine, initially agreeing such things in civil law contracts. If the overwhelming majority of citizens behave well by their own motivation and insight, the state can, as *final* authority, compel the few who do not wish to behave well to do so. As long as we conceive of the state as it is today, as involved in economic interests and educational tasks, the current method of passing laws seems necessary and justified. But the more we succeed in regulating education and balancing economic interests outside the state, the more the state can become a pure 'rights state' in accordance with its intrinsic nature. It is this concept of the state that Steiner invokes when he links the terms 'state' and 'rights'.

7.3 Threefolding as the basis for democracy

We have adopted many legal terms from the Romans. The first Romans were lawless, unwanted men, who also stole unmarried maidens to be their wives. Roman law addressed lower human passions, and today it is still partly true to say that there are people who would do wrong if it were not for legal compulsion; and for this reason we continue to need laws. But for the law's further development we need to develop democratic forms of organisation that do not stifle our sense of justice. If we have nothing more than the old legal compulsion, then antisocial ways of behaving will be exacerbated and will need still stricter laws to control them.

By contrast, threefolding leads to organisational forms that facilitate and cultivate in each of us a sense of our rights and obligations. Steiner's comments about the state and democracy are still entirely valid today:

> If states are to become democracies, they must enable human beings to bring to expression what governs and regulates the relationship between all responsible adults. And every responsible adult must share equally in this regulation. Administration and representation must express what arises in a person's awareness simply by virtue of being a healthy, responsible person ... If a true democracy is to be formed out of a state as it has been hitherto, then one will have to remove from it and make a matter for full self-regulation everything which only a particular human being's individual development can elaborate with the right impulses. This cannot be regulated simply by being an adult citizen. The social circumstances that every adult citizen is competent to judge are the legal relationships between people. At the same time these are the conditions of life that can maintain their social character only because in democratic institutions they manifest a collective will arising from the real interplay of individual human wills.[4]

Equality before the law requires recognition of the human being as a spiritual being who belongs to the world of spirit as much as to the earthly world.

> You see a democracy is of no use at all unless it is based on the right estimation of human beings, one which can really only be fully inscribed in the human soul by a science of the spirit. Democracy always contains the potential for its own downfall

if it does not, at the same time, contain the seed of
real esteem for the human being.[5]

Steiner describes the dangers of democracy in dramatic
terms:

> Let us assume that democracy is the ideal of
> social co-existence. But if we tried to introduce
> this democracy somewhere, it would inevitably
> ultimately lead to its own destruction. The tendency
> of democracy is inevitably such that, when the
> democrats are together, one person is always
> endeavouring to overpower the other, always
> trying to secure entitlement at the other's expense.
> This goes without saying. It strives towards its
> own dissolution. So if you introduce democracy
> somewhere, it may appear very fine in theory. In
> reality, however, democracy will lead to the opposite
> of democracy as inevitably as a pendulum swings
> one way and then the other. This is simply an
> inevitable part of life. Democracies will always, after
> a time, die from their own democratic nature.[6]

> Democracies can only emerge in the right way on
> a legal basis if those in democratic parliaments
> enshrine in law what lives in the relationship of one
> person to another as equals.[7]

> Today we have arrived at the point where we
> must ask, since democracy must inevitably arise,
> how we can realise it in practice. This can only be
> done in fact by placing it on its own foundation,
> and by separating out from it, to one side or the
> other, what cannot be democratically administered
> because it cannot be judged by all people.[8]

On one side and the other a government must be a relinquishing one, directing cultural life towards its own administration on the one hand, and economic life into its own on the other.[9]

The first step towards doing this is by democracy permitting free initiatives and arrangements. Today anyone can recognise the validity of this as a general principle. But people only acknowledge the benefit of the state withdrawing from the economy and cultural life once these free initiatives exist and have proven themselves to be viable and sustainable.

Today government spending – the proportion of state and state-associated economic activity in the overall economy – is between 40 and 50 per cent in many developed countries (UK 48.5%, USA 41.6%, Switzerland 33.8%, Russia 35.8%, Germany 45.4%, Sweden 51.2%).[10] There is a widespread belief that solidarity in the economy, the development of a strong economy, can only be achieved by a strong government that intervenes in economic matters. In the economic realm the state is assigned three major tasks.

1. It should ensure provision of 'public goods' that everyone needs but not everyone can afford, such as roads.
2. It should ensure just incomes that the economy itself does not create.
3. It should influence the business cycle and combat economic crises by administering money and public investments.

These views are connected with a sense that governments are more reasonable than individual, 'fundamentally egotistic' people, and that no society would be just if the state and its laws did not ensure it. Since the Enlightenment it is true that people have become individually responsible, and that all are equally involved in determining rights and laws. But in many realms we do not trust people's maturity or responsibility, and think that they must be overseen by governments. Even in a democracy we regard the state as a higher authority; and this authoritarian state is misused by political parties and lobbyists to secure the most varied partisan interests. By contrast, threefolding urges us to undertake organisation of the economy from the grass roots, or in other words to build it up from people themselves and their enterprises. There are many examples that show this is possible.[11]

People themselves – and by no means just those with anthroposophical outlooks – are seeking and finding new solutions for problems in society. However, anthroposophy can help to shed light on the significance of these initiatives. Threefolding develops democracy in two ways.

Only through threefolding does the *great democratic ideal in its broadest sense* become possible since it helps people to come into their own in all fields where they work responsibly. Threefolding replaces the sovereignty of the people, an abstract concept, with the sovereignty of each individual. In every distinct but connected system of the social order people are sovereign in different ways: in the state through democratic decisions, in the economy through contractually regulated collaboration, and in cultural life through the free acknowledgment of individual skills and abilities.

Democracy *in the narrower sense* is increasingly vanishing in many countries that call themselves democracies. It can only be realised where the state concerns itself with nothing other than the justice that is the same for all.

7.4 The economic aspect of the state

Even if a government does nothing more than ensure universal equal human rights, it still participates in the economy, and does so exclusively as a consuming entity. For this it needs money which people supply to the state in the form of taxes. The methods and principles of taxation are a hotly debated political issue today. They become far less contentious once social threefolding is implemented since the sum of state taxes can then be far less than at present. But lowering taxes is not the first thing we should do, since at the moment the state still needs all the money it receives in this way to meet its large-scale social and cultural obligations. Lowering of taxes will follow as a consequence of our increasing ability to take in hand the social and cultural tasks that currently are left for the state to deal with, and do so without waiting for new state laws and administrations.

Today, state administration is also partly run by business corporations that not only produce yields but also give rise to costs. These are businesses whose task in the past was regarded as serving the whole population without necessarily producing a profit. Today many of them are being 'privatised' so that the state can slim itself down. Underlying this is a justified concern that seems to be heading in the direction of threefolding: these productive state operations ought also to be run in an entrepreneurial and autonomous way. And yet this is being attempted in a manner very far removed from threefolding. It is claimed and believed – it has become a real dogma – that entrepreneurial activity primarily exists to make profit. The operations that are suitable for this aim are selected and 'privatised', and privatisation is seen as synonymous with profit-making. Usually the form of a share-holding company is chosen since financiers are willing to provide money to purchase a state-run operation if they make a profit from it. In fact this is all very small-minded. The entrepreneurial character of the economy is much more wide-ranging and interesting than mere profit-seeking, since the human spirit works into the economy through entrepreneurial initiative. As threefolding sees it, the state should indeed relinquish its productive businesses in a way that enables entrepreneurial initiative to come to full expression, yet without losing an orientation to the common good in the process.

If we now consider the slimmed-down state as threefolding sees it, we have to solve the question of how best to tax, which taxes can be abolished and where in the economy taxes should be levied. Taxes as 'compulsory gifts' serve to pay the material costs of state administration and provide an income for those who work in it. If everything of an economically productive nature is increasingly relinquished by the state, those working in state administration become 'pure consumers'. Financing of the state by means of credit as pure consumer credit is in many cases absurd since state debts shift responsibility for expenditure into the future, and it must then still be paid for out of taxes.

If a state administration only participates in economic consumption, it seems logically consistent and illuminating that Steiner proposed a consumption tax as the only form of taxation:

> A consumption tax must be created; that is,
> someone who spends a lot of money must naturally
> be taxed more than someone who does not need
> very much, since if someone puts their money under
> the mattress this has no importance for society. It
> only acquires importance when it is spent.[12]

This consumption tax would be levied on every single person simply as a person, since the state is concerned with the legal security and protection of all human beings.[13] Rudolf Steiner did not speak only of consumption tax but also of expenditure tax, which must always be levied when money is spent since only then does the money received become active in the productive economy.[14] Every expenditure is a stimulus for the economy to produce another such item as has been bought. Consumption is what every person contributes to economic life as a consumer. If someone does not spend their money, it remains ineffective and of no significance for the rest of society. Consumption makes needs apparent, and production can then orient itself accordingly. When the state levies taxation and participates in this consumption, it should do so in an entirely neutral way. Steiner therefore wished people to pay taxes proportionally to the amount of money they spent. He expressly rejected indirect taxation, which are taxes added to the price of goods. Companies factor all tax levied in the production process into their price calculations, and thereby try to foist this on the consumer. This is also true of VAT or sales tax, though this has the advantage that it can be largely managed in a competitively neutral way, and is separately indicated, and thus acts as a general taxation on consumption.[15]

Nowadays there is a greater focus on environmental impact and use of natural resources than was necessary in Steiner's day. There is a clear case for the taxation of fossil fuels since everyone uses them, and in their use air is also consumed. Many models of ecological tax reform are currently being discussed, and to some small degree these already exist and are being realised. These taxes too result in costs for companies.

It is not clear from these considerations exactly what pure consumption and expenditure taxation would look like. Nor did Steiner comment on how such tax should actually be levied. He gave the reason for this in a lecture in 1919:

> You see, there is for instance an optimum taxation system. But there is no point at all in working out this optimum taxation system conceptually; instead we should work towards a threefold approach. As this is increasingly realised, and through this very threefold activity itself, the best taxation system will arise within the social organism. We have to create the conditions under which the best social

arrangements can come about. There is no value or reality in theoretically elaborating the optimum way to do things.[16]

In specific situations it will become apparent that there are various possibilities with their advantages and disadvantages, from which people will choose the tax system they consider most just. The principles that govern such decisions are the important thing. A tax on profit applies taxation in the production domain by taxing sums that leave the economy and are allocated to profit distribution. But profit also contains donations to cultural life and social welfare which ought not to be taxed. If someone funds donations or loans from their income, they ought not to be taxed on this. Only when the money is spent by its recipients as purchase money does it become liable to expenditure tax; and that would be taxation applicable solely to purchase money.

8. Economics and Law in the School Curriculum

8.1 Overcoming dogmas

There are many textbooks on citizenship, law and economics; and as a teacher one is tempted to use them, but is surprised and dismayed to discover dogmas and prejudices on almost every page. These dogmas are taught and promulgated in schools, colleges and the daily media, and profoundly inform our whole way of thinking and even our modes of speech.

It makes sense to include law and economics as distinct subjects in the school curriculum, where we should also examine prevailing dogmas. But before the age of 15, adolescents are unlikely to have much interest in such issues. In the whole of a child's education up to 14, we cannot speak about law and economics in a technical sense, nor is any separate 'subject' necessary for this. What is important, though, is for pupils to experience aspects of rights and economy in every school subject and in the whole life of a school. If these do not live in concepts that accord with reality but instead in dogmas which, in particular exert their unconscious, negative effect in our habits of speech, pupils will simply absorb them in their turn in this form. Teachers should therefore try to overcome their own customary habits of thoughts and speech in these areas, and this book can help here. But what we ourselves learn theoretically as adults, and seek to apply in our life, cannot simply be passed on to children in the same form.

In his fundamental work *Towards Social Renewal*, Steiner formulated the task as follows:

> The present crisis in humanity requires each one of us to develop certain sensibilities. Stimulus for such sensibilities must be given through education in the same way as the four processes are taught in arithmetic.[1]

In a lecture he elaborated further on this:

> Nowadays we are thought uneducated if we don't know our multiplication tables or anything else that belongs to general education. But we are not regarded as uneducated if we have no social awareness or live in the social organism as if asleep. This really has to change in future – and it will if people come to see that the most elementary schooling should include equipping oneself with a social will in the same way as one nowadays equips oneself with knowledge of arithmetic. Today everyone is supposed to know what three times three is. In future it will seem no more difficult than this to know how capital interest relates to ground rent – to pick on something important in modern life. In future this will appear of no greater difficulty than knowing three times three is nine. But such knowledge will provide a foundation for playing a healthy part in the social organism – in other words, for a healthier society in general.[2]

Social awareness, children's feelings and will, are deeply influenced by everything we say and do. If we have realistic ideas about work, value, money, possessions and property, we will already tell stories in kindergarten in a very different way than if, for instance, our concept of money is entirely materialistic. Likewise the way we speak of fractions and percentages will be affected by this. We should not convey theories to the children but describe phenomena as they are. This is similar to science, where we can do much harm by starting science teaching from preconceived models rather than carefully attending to observation of phenomena, and seeking to discover natural laws as they emerge from these phenomena themselves. Observing phenomena is not something devoid of thought. We have to understand them too, for otherwise we merely gaze at them. But we do not understand them if we try to explain them with a theory rather than by what is inherent in them. Explaining is different from understanding.

One goal of education is that we do not use a world without understanding it. In relation to technology Rudolf Steiner said:

> We live in a world created by human beings,
> formed by human thoughts: we use it without
> understanding it. This fact, that we understand
> nothing of things that human beings have formed,
> which are basically the outcome of human thoughts,
> is of great significance for people's overall mood
> of soul and spirit. They have to numb themselves
> really, so that they do not perceive the effects caused
> by this ... The worst thing is to experience the
> world made by human beings without concerning
> oneself with this world.[3]

This applies not only to technology, but also to the social domain. Not to understand the world we live in is unendurable. This is one aspect that plays a part in the relationship between schooling and practical life. On the other hand, it is equally unendurable to know what human beings and nature need and not to act on it. The first is a deficiency of knowledge and the second a deficiency of will. A school does not exist to convey knowledge for the sake of knowledge, or so that our knowledge invests us with a sense of superiority, but so that we acquire knowledge that we can apply in a social context. It is important for children to experience that their school is not isolated from society. It must be utterly a school, and dedicate itself exclusively to education, and for that very reason forge connections with farms, businesses and social tasks. There is an ever-increasing sense of this necessity in many places today, and many schools are doing exemplary work through their social and ecological approaches and by sending students to do practical work in businesses and social projects.

8.2 The child's path into economic life

By nature, children live in a pure gift economy. Unless externally compelled to do so, it is foreign to their nature to think they should give something in return for what they receive, or should be rewarded for what they do. They do not compare economic values in mutual exchange and calculation. Until the beginning of puberty, or at least up to the age of 11, monetary figures should not be assigned to economic values. A pound of wheat is valuable because one can bake bread with it to feed and nourish people. Since we adults are so accustomed to valuing things in monetary terms, we should try to remember, as has been emphasised here, that this is not a primary value.

Only from age 12 can monetary examples be included in arithmetic, though not initially in an abstract, academic context. The market is not a mechanism between supply, demand and price, but rather a place where goods are exchanged and traded. Interest calculations, too, should not be treated as a theoretical law functioning as a mechanism, but should always be placed in the context of actual mutual human engagement, using real-life examples.

Mathematical and economic calculations are not the same as each other. Percentages are pure mathematics and should be understood and practised as such. Interest calculations, on the other hand, must always be placed in a social context. Then we can also understand conditions in medieval times when Christians were forbidden from lending money at interest. Jews likewise were prohibited from doing this in relation to other Jews, but were allowed to do so to people of other faiths. As money lenders they fulfilled a necessary function at the time, as many people were dependent on borrowing money against pledged goods.

The practical question as to how work and payment are connected surfaces early on in a young person's life. Here it is important for children to have experienced the importance of collaboration. If they help out at home or have a small task to do at school, their work is only valuable as part of a whole, and has no isolated significance. Likewise it is good to realise that what they receive in the way of food, clothing and so on arises through many people's collaboration. Children should experience, and be repeatedly reminded of the great value of collaboration, and the fact that it underlies almost all economic activity. A time arrives when young people want to earn money themselves (though it is good not to do this before the age of 12). To be precise about it, they want to be sole traders, since in this scenario work and payment are directly connected. One should keep reminding young people that they are offering a service and, if this is wanted and needed, they can ask for a *quid pro quo*, a price. They are not 'employed' and rather than receiving a 'wage', they receive reciprocation for something they have made or done that is needed and can be used. An exchange of service against 'consideration' is not a matter of work but of enterprise. Young people who look for a small job are in the position of a sole trader or entrepreneur. If a whole group of young people offer their services because they want to fund a festival or a trip, they earn a sum together which they likewise spend together or divide between them.

Teaching children about the Industrial Revolution at age 14 is the best opportunity to use tangible examples to illustrate the division of labour, labour as commodity, the misery caused by the 'labour market', the tasks of the entrepreneur and the meaning of capital. The great economic crash of the 1920s is a good basis for studying the legal forms of companies. Rights, laws and economic conditions should play a major part in the study of history. Descriptions should always be as vivid and concrete as possible. Law and economics are integral to life skills. All teaching concerned with life skills (and what lesson is not?) contributes to an understanding of laws, rights and economics.

8.3 Money as bookkeeping

Bookkeeping is the very best way of giving people a tangible experience of the nature of money. Every till receipt is a bit of bookkeeping, and shows us how much we have spent and on what. Bookkeeping involves making written records of monetary processes. Money enables us to comprehend economic processes in numerical figures, and in bookkeeping these figures become clearly apparent. Above all in the balance sheet, bookkeeping can also be misused to conceal the truth. Nevertheless, numerical figures themselves can in principle always enable us to distinguish truth from deception although this is not always easy because things are complex. If, in addition, we learn to distinguish between purchase money, loan money and gift money, the concept of money becomes differentiated and interesting.

From age 12 onwards, it makes sense to undertake simple

bookkeeping in the form of income and expenditure accounts. Separately from this one can also record assets and liabilities and thereby distinguish the different qualities of purchase money and loan money. It was a brilliant invention of traders in northern Italy during the Renaissance to combine these two separate calculations into double-entry bookkeeping. No young person should leave school without having practised and thus in principle understood this invention. Experience has shown that this can be done from age 16. Here it is also possible, and necessary, to speak about land, labour and capital as production factors, in order to understand that all three of these are distinct and separate from bookkeeping. Labour must not be a cost factor, and if land and capital are listed as assets in the balance sheet, one should remember that these are productivity values as we tried to demonstrate in the sections on labour, land and capital.

8.4 Work experience in industry and agriculture

Work experience on organically run farms, a key aspect of the curriculum in Steiner-Waldorf Schools in Classes 9, 10 and 11 (age 14–17), gives young people insight into the nature of this area of the economy. It is quite different in industry. Working on machines to which the human being is harnessed can initially be an unpleasant shock to the system: 'I'm never going to do anything like that!' Young people who react in this way are quite right. It is wrong for people to spend a full working week engaged in such work. If the aim of such a work placement is to help young people understand industry, then in school lessons, in specific examples, it is important first to study how valuable products are created through technology, division of labour and collaboration. These sequences and connections can be very complex, but in principle they can always be clearly comprehended because the human mind has conceived and planned them. This is a fact to be considered when organising work experiences and educational trips. The foundations must be laid in lessons where in many examples, young people can always understand how technical facilities work. This counteracts their insecurity if they feel that technology is beyond their grasp.

Living creatures and organisms are a quite different matter, for here we must always consider how such creatures react. Something mysterious and incomprehensible always remains. First you do something, then you have to stand back and await further developments, and be present again at the right moment to intervene once more. This is intrinsic to the caring professions, and young people can experience it in work with children, the elderly or people with disabilities. However, to undertake this kind of educational or therapeutic work they need to be older. They can participate in agriculture at an earlier age, and this is why children in Waldorf schools do gardening from Class 6 (age 11–12), where they encounter and cultivate living organisms. Later they can experience the social aspects of this when doing practical work on a farm. Experience has shown that Class 10 or 11 (age 16–17) is the best time for this, as they have acquired sufficient maturity for the social aspects involved.

In agriculture there is also much that is related to industry which must be understood. The use of machine capital per workplace is greater in agriculture than in most sectors of industry. The productivity of labour has greatly increased over the last decades in agriculture through the use of machines, freeing many people from work on the land. But crops, and animals above all, are still dependent on manual cultivation and human care. We have to relate much more strongly to animals than to material objects. Young people can witness this best of all in the cowshed, where cattle have to be fed and milked twice a day even at the weekend. In modern free-stall pens, it has been found that calves and cattle run wild if they are never led by a halter by human hands.

Mechanical industrial labour is something we undertake because we wish to achieve an aim determined by human reason and intent. In agriculture (and in other caring professions) we work because living creatures or organisms need our help. Working with the living world addresses our will, whereas machine work calls upon our intellect – with whose aid we have constructed our machines and organised their sequences. We continually have to summon our will to engage in the effort of physical work in nature. (Farmers have all experienced how no such effort is needed when they're sitting on a tractor since the machine itself carries them along, and only when they get down from it, do they notice how tired they are.)

In lectures for teachers Rudolf Steiner placed great importance on noting the oppositeness between thinking and will. With our thinking and picturing capacity we grasp what has arisen from the past, while will relates to the future that lies in the will as potential. This germinal quality is lacking wherever machines relieve us of our work and effort. Machines intervene between us and nature. Shortly before the Waldorf School was founded, Steiner spoke in drastic terms about the meaning of work.[4] The machine is entirely transparent for the intellect, but this means:

> That the human will oriented to the machine is not in truth oriented to anything real. Basically, the machine is a chimera for the all-embracing reality of the world. And industrialism introduces into our life something that renders the will meaningless in a higher sense.

By 'higher sense' Steiner means looking at larger cosmic relationships in which our present life on earth is embedded.

When a farmer ploughs a furrow with a horse harnessed to the plough, this work with a horse, in which natural powers are still at work, has meaning above and beyond the immediate present – it has a cosmic meaning. When a wasp constructs its nest, this wasp's nest has a cosmic meaning. When someone strikes a spark from a flint, then kindles tinder, using this to light a fire, he is connected with nature, and this has cosmic meaning. Modern industrialism has removed us from this connection and meaning. There is no cosmic meaning when we turn on our electric lights ... and if you enter a modern factory with its machines, this is a kind of hole in the cosmos and has no significance for cosmic evolution. If you go into the forest and collect wood, this has cosmic significance above and beyond earthly evolution *per se*.

This does not mean of course that we should abolish machines and return to a primitive way of life. But we can take any opportunity to do work by hand, as is certainly possible and necessary in agriculture, forestry and many caring professions. We ought to drastically reduce the time we spend working at computers or in factories, and money must be managed in a way that enables this caring, manual work to be done to a greater degree. Industrial labour, though, which intrinsically has no meaning for the will, must acquire a meaning that we ourselves give it. This is possible if 'we raise ourselves to a worldview that gives meaning to what is meaningless – let's call it industrialism – by drawing this meaning from the spirit; by saying, we seek tasks that originate in the spirit.'[5]

That is why, in Chapter 4 on capital, we stressed the importance of every business enterprise placing itself in the service of an idea, a meaningful purpose.

Appendix

Mutual Credit Clearing: Riegel and Greco

Throughout the world national governments have made it their prerogative to create and issue money. In any area of national jurisdiction we are obliged to use such currency as the legally prescribed means of payment. This has many advantages in daily use; and anyway, we are so used to it that we cannot easily conceive of any other money system. Nevertheless, attempts are repeatedly made to think of an alternative, and two American thinkers are of particular interest here.

E. C. Riegel (1879–1954) wrote several books – now long out of print – in the first half of the twentieth century, when economic and finance crises were showing how unstable the prevailing monetary system is. Few know of Riegel any more, and even specialists in financial issues do not engage with his ideas, but you can find his works on the internet. He proposed separating the economic exchange process from political interests and from the banks' business interests. This would, he said, be possible if private participants in the economy, rather than the state and the banks, created money through their expenditure and income, and brought it into circulation. In today's money system, governments and banks collaborate in a way that invests them with great power. This system was first used in England when William of Orange waged war on Louis XIV of France, and needed money to do so. He obtained this as bank loans, and in return for the favour gave the Bank of England, founded in 1694, the right to print and issue bank notes. The Bank of England later became the model for central issuing banks which were established in practically every country in the world, with the privilege of increasing the quantity of money in circulation in the political interests of the government and in the business interests of the banks.

This prerogative is regularly used if a government wants to wage war and is equipping itself militarily. This inflation of money supply leads sooner or later to a reduction in the value of money, and to higher prices; and so one can say that the money governments have obtained for themselves through credit harms the economy. The state monopoly on money is by far the state's greatest intervention in the economy. Riegel believed that the change to the money system proposed by him was the most important foundation for any possibility of peace and freedom in human society.

Thomas H. Greco (born 1936) states that Riegel has been his biggest influence. He wrote four books and many articles, concerning himself not just theoretically but also in thoroughly practical ways with the question of how state money can be replaced by private communities organising their monetary transactions themselves by establishing clearing systems. Greco's four books are:
  Money and Debt: A Solution to the Global Crisis (1990)
  New Money for Healthy Communities (1994)
  Money: Understanding and Creating Alternatives to Legal Tender (2001)
  The End of Money and the Future of Civilization (2009)

The last title should be obligatory reading for anyone who wants to gain deeper theoretical and practical insight into the economy. These two authors are largely unknown in German-speaking countries, and I only encountered them in 2014, a year after this present book was first published in German. I discovered with surprise and pleasure that their ideas to a large degree concur with those I had elaborated from Rudolf Steiner's theory of money. In his ground-breaking book of 1919, *Towards Social Renewal*, Steiner had urged that the state should have nothing to do with the endorsement of money. He made some further comments – but did not develop them in detail – about what money arising within the economy itself could look like. Nor did students and interpreters of Steiner elaborate further on this separation of money and the state. Anthroposophists can take little pride in the fact that American thinkers have overtaken them and done the work awaiting them. Riegel and Greco seem to have been unaware of Steiner's book *Towards Social Renewal* although Edith Maryon translated it into English in 1919 already, the year it first appeared.

Below I will summarise some, though by no means all of the ideas contained in *The End of Money*. Greco's title refers to the fact that money today is no longer a 'thing' but must instead be seen purely as an information system. Like Steiner, Greco says money is nothing more than bookkeeping: 'Money is merely an accounting system' (p. 116).

When money consisted of gold and silver coins, it could be seen as a thing or commodity. Nowadays money consists only of bank assets arising from credit issued by banks. If someone takes out a loan he becomes, firstly, a debtor of the bank; at the same time he also receives money into an account from which he can pay bills. Monetary circulation functions as the transfer from one account to another, thus through clearing. This is true not only of direct clearing communities such as LETS but also in the clearing system managed by banks. There is an important difference however: at the outset of the monetary process and before financial transactions begin, the banks create money through credit given to the loan recipient. They levy interest on this credit, and profit from it. Instead of this, in a community of purchasers and vendors, we can mutually grant each other interest-free credit. In clearing unions or communities (e.g. LETS) it is always a matter of the calculation (clearing) of debts (which we accrue through purchase) and credit (which we receive when we sell something or receive money). This is why Greco speaks of 'mutual credit clearing'. This functions without someone having to create money in advance. Banks are still behaving as if money were a 'thing' that must first be created before it can be used in financial transactions.

By means of a system of direct clearing of income and expenditure, today's banking system and its money creation would become superfluous, and money creation by public debt would likewise be overcome ('Direct clearing makes conventional money and banking obsolete' p. 122).

Like Riegel, Greco also sees centralism as the greatest danger facing the world. In the USA, over lengthy arguments and debates, the central banking system developed on the Bank of England model. This led to the American administration being able to incur debt with the banks to a degree it can never repay through tax incomes. By this means it was able to procure the money necessary for waging war; and the central banking system today remains the basis for the global power underpinning the 'new world order'. Through state indebtedness the quantity of money was greatly increased and gave rise to dollar devaluation in recent decades, with resulting damage to the real economy.

To characterise money, Greco also resorts to the image of wave movements through time (p. 118). In the clearing accountancy of purchases and sales, the account of an individual participant fluctuates between debit and credit. In the money system as a whole, the debts of one participant are balanced by the assets of an other. In clearing communities or unions, every member is allocated an overdraft limit that corresponds to his regular income or takings. According to Greco, this is usually based on a three-month period.

Greco places great emphasis on distinguishing rigorously between exchange and financing functions. Credit is needed for both, but this is short-term credit in the case of *exchange* (monetary transactions) and long-term for *capital*-creating *finance*. Short-term 'credit clearing' continually creates new money. Creation of capital, on the other hand, which exists in order to renew or increase the means of production, is based on money already being available, and being transferred from savers to entrepreneurs (pp. 66f). Greco therefore concludes that capital investments must be financed by savings rather than by the creation of new money (p. 243):

> Those of us who have a surplus that we are able
> to save provide the resources needed by others to
> become more productive. In a developed economy
> in which there is specialisation of labour, saving
> is essentially a social phenomenon ... Saving and
> investment are two sides of the same coin. (p. 245).

Thus Greco distinguishes between money as a means of payment and as capital for investment by the different lengths of time that credit lasts. This is similar to the distinction Steiner makes between purchase money and loan money. However, Steiner bases his views on what one can do with money (buying, lending, giving) – or in other words, how one can behave towards others via money. He thus characterises money as a relationship between people. From the point of view of an individual who lends money to another, purchase money appears to be changed into loan money. In reality, the purchase money's existence continues, though now in the hand or on the account of the loan money recipient; and the loan money credit (or one can also say the 'money capital') arises as something new and additional.

The third kind of money described by Steiner is gift money, and here he sheds the right light on the very great economic importance of giving. This distinction between money types is connected with social threefolding. Purchase money as means of payment and liquidity is a matter of economics. Capital, by contrast, belongs to cultural life: as loan money it exists so that capacities can be used; and as gift money it can facilitate the development of capacities or abilities.

Greco likewise distinguishes 'three types of economic interaction' (p. 101):

◊ Gifts
◊ Involuntary transfers, such as theft, robbery, extortion or taxes
◊ Reciprocal exchange

In terms of economics, the first two are the same, that is, one-sided transfers. They are distinguished only as regards law and power. The question of the power connected with money is one that especially concerns Greco, and Riegel too. Steiner is more precise in the way he distinguishes the three types of money, because he defines them in purely economic terms, and does not muddle economics with law.

Based on his practical experiences as an association consultant, Greco describes in detail how clearing unions can be established, what conditions are needed for this and why it is relatively common for such initiatives to fail after initial success. Clearing unions or communities must be small-scale and easily comprehensible, and network inter-regionally with other such communities. This federalist structure is an important foundation for sustainable economics ('The credit clearing exchange is the key element that enables a community to develop a sustainable economy under local control and to maintain a high standard of living and quality of life,' p. 196). Greco envisages a structure developing from below upwards from local clearing communities. Small groups that agree on their shared principles ('affinity groups') can form such clearing communities, which can then interact with other groups to produce inter-group trading:

> The structure that I envision consists of local mutual credit clearing exchanges comprised of small affinity groups that are networked regionally and, eventually, globally. Affinity groups that are small and co-responsible enable high levels of trust and democratic self-regulation, but they interact with other affinity groups in ways that enable intergroup trading and the development of social solidarity. (p. 231).

As we saw in Chapter 1, Bernard Lietaer also proposed establishing clearing systems, though only as complementary currencies alongside state currencies. He even assumed as a given that there would be three major international currencies in existence: the euro, the dollar and a supranational currency for Asia. Greco, on the other hand, wants to prevent and overcome these developments, which are a part of the 'new world order' and thus governed by the global banking elite. He sees direct credit clearing as a revolutionary innovation that can change the world (p. 192).

Definition of the 'measure of value' plays an important role. Usually one says that money has three functions: as a means of exchange, a means of value retention and as a measure of value. As well as separating the first two, payment transactions and capital, from each other, Greco also differentiates these from the measure of value. He says that no existing money should be a measure of value but rather that the latter must be one against which every existing form of money can be measured. Greco therefore proposes a shopping basket containing 12 to 15 commodities, traded in free markets, that are important in world trade, that meet basic human needs, have relatively stable prices, and are of a quality that can be standardised (p. 276). The measure of value is the unit of account and clearing unit.

However, this is not the same as the *value basis* of money. If the value of a currency is defined by a shopping basket of goods, this does not mean that these goods are deposited somewhere (like gold in a bank) and that one can convert money into these goods in the sense of 'currency security'. Rather, there is only a settlement or clearing of service or commodity against service or commodity, and here *monetary value* is the clearing standard. The *basis of monetary transaction* is economic performance. Temporary debts that I incur when purchasing in a clearing community are balanced by me when I myself sell goods and services, including my receipt of wages.

Notes

Note: Works by Rudolf Steiner without page references are cited with their 'CW' (Collected Works) number where published English translations exist. Where page references are given in the original, or where no translations exist, references are to the German edition of Steiner's works, referred to as 'GA' (Gesamt Ausgabe). Quotations from works or lectures by Rudolf Steiner have been retranslated for this edition.

1. Money Created in the Economy

1 An exception to this is Budd, *Finance at the Threshold.*
2 Robertson, *Future Money: Breakdown or Breakthrough?* Huber & Robertson, *Creating New Money.*
3 Graeber, *Debt: The First 5000 Years,* particularly Chapter 2, The Myth of Barter. In his book, drawing on extensive historical research, Graeber demonstrates that the most ancient money systems were *credit systems.* This is correct insofar as credit initially signifies trust, and only gradually came to be associated with defined repayments and interest. The oldest forms of credit are not loans but gifts. Transitional forms between the two also existed.
4 The German word *Gold* is very close to *Geld,* the word for money. [Tr.]
5 (GA 190, lecture of March 3, 1919, p. 25) stated: 'Gold only has monetary value because it gradually acquired the status amongst humankind of an especially loved commodity. People agreed with one another to accord gold special esteem ... The value of gold depends solely on the tacit agreement between people to see gold as valuable ... In reality, gold has only an apparent value. You cannot eat gold. However rich in gold you are, you cannot live from it unless someone gives you something for it. It relies on nothing but this tacit human agreement ... But this seeming value assigned to a particular metal will cease if one hands over administration of money to the body economic, so that the state no longer has any hand in regulating it.'

6 See 'Money creation' at www.wikipedia.org.

7 North, *A Short History of Money.*

8 We are speaking here of a conceptual abstraction. This is different from the real abstraction that underlies money by virtue of the fact that it has no intrinsic commodity value. Only *this* attribute of money allows the value of every possible commodity or service to be expressed in terms of money. This is also true of gold which, while having a commodity value, can only become money if it is acknowledged as a universal, abstract means of exchange.

9 Binswanger, *Money and Magic,* and Lietaer, *The Mystery of Money.*

10 Lietaer, *The Future of Money.*

11 Keynes, J.M. *Collected Writings,* Vol. XXV.

12 GA 23, p. 129.

13 GA 337a, lecture of May 30, 1919, p. 78.

14 While different technical solutions are possible to distinguish purchase money and loan money, the important thing is to distinguish them clearly. In his fantasy tale, *Rare Albion – Further Adventures of the Wizard of Oz,* Budd designates the two kinds of money 'yellow money' and 'blue money' and has them administered by two different kinds of bank. In his new book, *Finance at the Threshold,* he distinguishes cash und credit, demanding that they be kept separate (Ch. 10.2, De-linking cash and credit). Once we are aware that money is nothing more than book-keeping, then 'money emission and credit creation' can be instigated by anyone. Budd calls this 'citizenised central banking'.

15 Every invoice carries a payment term, for instance, of 30 days. Until it is paid, a debt exists. An account must list creditors and debtors, and calculate all short-term obligations and credits in relation to purchase money.

16 Compare Gaedeke, 'Geld und Gelderkenntnis' in *Sozialwissenschaftliches Forum,* Vol. 3, pp. 94ff.

17 CW 340, *Economics, the World as one Economy,* lecture of Aug 4, 1922.

18 Gesell, *The Natural Economic Order.*

19 There is extensive literature on depreciative money. A brief account can be found in Senf, *Die blinden Flecken der Ökonomie,* pp. 191ff. This view is somewhat modified in See Kennedy, Lietaer & Rogers, *People Money.*

20 Herrmannstorfer, *Pseudo Market,* p. 104.

21 GA 23, pp. 132f.

22 GA 331, discussion, evening of June 24, 1919, pp. 187ff.

23 GA 23, p. 115.

24 GA 340, p. 58.

25 GA 340, lecture of Aug 6, 1922, pp. 209f.

26 This was just how the people around W.E. Barkhoff proceeded in their innovative development of new monetary institutions. Rolf Kerler describes vividly how they always started from practical needs and possibilities, and at the same time looked to the big, fundamental goals. These were the same goals as we have been describing in this chapter.

27 Huber & Robertson, *Creating New Money*.

28 Friedrich Hayek, *Denationalization of Money: An Analysis of the Theory and Practice of Concurrent Currencies* (Hobart Papers), Institute of Economic Affairs, 1977; also available on mises.org/books/denationalisation.pdf

29 See Budd, *Finance at the Threshold*, p. 71. As an expert on corporate finance, Budd proceeds from actual realities; and these show us that the corporate finance world as it has so far operated, cannot continue in the same way in future. It stands at the edge of an abyss. Beyond this threshold only an entirely different type of economy can lead us forwards. The precondition for this is that monetary processes are examined without prejudice and much more carefully than has so far happened. Here, as Budd's book shows in detail, Rudolf Steiner's ideas and suggestions on monetary theory are an indispensable foundation. By other routes, Budd arrives at outcomes that very largely agree with the content of this present volume.

2. Labour and Income

1 GA 34, p. 213. See also the lecture of March 12, 1908, 'Profession and Income' in GA 56, pp. 227ff.

2 The terms 'value 1' and 'value 2' in Steiner's *World Economy* must be understood as processes and functions. The first value is a function of nature and work. A thousand spoons are worth more than ten because more natural materials and labour must be used to make them. The second 'value' involves intelligent considerations of how the necessary work can be reduced – that is, the human mind increases the productivity of work. This is true of all work, but especially apparent in the division of labour in large-scale production. When the goods arrive in the shops (where different factors are at play) a single spoon can become cheaper. The second 'value' is a negative one compared with the positive first value.

3 Among other places, in GA 79, p. 261, GA 337b, p. 226. In GA 23, p. 131 *(Towards Social Renewal)*, a similar formulation is used in an author's

note in describing the true price, though without using the term 'primal cell'. In this connection, see also Section 2.10 of this book.

4 GA 79, pp. 246f.

5 Steiner, *World Economy* (CW 340), lecture of Aug 3, 1922.

6 GA 330, p. 96.

7 This is a very cautious estimate. Rudolf Steiner's view was much more drastic: 'If every human being performed his share of manual work everywhere on the earth – well not absolutely everyone but this is an ideal we can get close to – then no one would need to do more than three to four hours manual work a day, at most ... More than three to four hours of manual labour are not necessitated by factors at work in humanity's evolution but instead – and we can say this quite calmly, without any emotion, as a fully objective fact – by the countless idlers and people taking advantage of social benefits. These things must be considered in a completely clear-eyed and honest way.' (GA 192, pp. 140f.)

8 GA 158, p. 143.

9 GA 335, pp. 266f.

10 GA 342, p. 49.

11 In addition to this there is voluntary work within organisations and associations, and all types of help and support for relatives and friends, amounting on average to 7 hours' work per week done by every adult (according to figures from the Swiss federal department for statistics in 2010).

12 This has been elaborated by Desaules (in *A Human Response to Globalisation)* a successful entrepreneur who writes from practical experience. A thorough exploration of this theme is given in Budd, *Finance at the Threshold,* Chapter 11, 'Deep Accounting'.

13 GA 23, pp. 138f.

14 GA 79, pp. 261f.

15 GA 79, pp. 259f.

16 GA 23, pp. 128f.

17 GA 54, lecture of March 2, 1908, p. 100.

18 GA 23, pp. 19f.

19 GA 23, p. 128.

20 Genevieve Vaughan's writing can be found on her website at www.gift-economy.com.

3. The Administration of Land by the Cultural Sphere

1 GLS Bank (Gemeinschaftsbank für Leihen und Schenken, which translates as 'community bank for loans and gifts') was the first social and ecological bank in Germany. Barkhoff, *Wir können lieben, wen wir wollen*. Kerler, *Eine Bank* für *den Menschen*, offers a fine, authentic account of Barkhoff's work.

2 GA 327, pp. 237, 239.

3 The 'aims and purposes' of the company's articles are stated as follows: 'The company's research encompasses the social, operational and financial conditions supporting biodynamic agriculture, along with the foundations of this method of agriculture itself. The company's work will be based on Rudolf Steiner's anthroposophy. To fulfil these aims, the company can purchase agricultural land and premises and have these managed by third parties according to their guidelines.'

4 Groh and McFadden, *Farms of Tomorrow Revisited*.

5 In this model the connection between agriculture and consumers is especially close. Naturally this is not possible everywhere in the same form; but even if trading and processing companies intervene, a close and conscious connection can be established between agriculture and its end-product consumers. This is done in exemplary fashion, for instance, by the Swiss cotton trading company, Remei AG. With its bioRe production chain it ensures that the path of cotton goods from farmers in India and Tanzania through to the Swiss wholesaler COOP, is made comprehensible and transparent for all involved (www.remei.ch)

6 www.hofehlers.de (only in German).

7 www.weide-hardebek.de (only in German).

8 www.dannwisch.de (only in German) and Koepf & Plato, *Die biologisch-dynamische Wirtschaftsweise*, pp. 248ff.

9 I would like to thank all the farms mentioned here who received me warmly and openly, offering insights into their ways of working. I worked for seven years at Bauckhof Farm (1972–1979).

10 GA 196, p. 286.

11 GA 339, p. 72.

12 Karl-Martin Dietz, among others, has described the details of this idea and how it can function in *Dialogische Schulführung an Waldorfschulen*, and in *Produktivität und Empfänglichkeit*.

13 Jobst von Heynitz, a member of staff at the Seminar für freiheitliche Ordnung (free social order seminar) founded in 1957, believes that this form of land administration by the spiritual/cultural sphere of the

social organism can 'only apply to the land as a means of production for companies, but not to land in private use as dwelling place or leisure space'. Von Heinitz cites Rudolf Steiner's lecture of June 16, 1920 (GA 337a, pp. 195ff) where he spoke of 'land for human labour' (Jobst von Heinitz in 'Eigentum, die Frage nach der Sozialbindung des Eigentums an Boden und Unternehmen', in *Sozialwissenschaftliches Forum* Vol. 5, Stuttgart 2000, p. 75). But in the discussion following this lecture, Steiner stated: 'Here a person gets a dwelling place in the same way as he gets a wage, and this is in fact subject to what comes from the organisation of spiritual life' (GA 337a, p. 226). If what Jobst von Heinitz thinks is right, then everything would remain as it has been as regards privately owned land. But in fact there are now a great many projects in the field of housing ownership in particularly, which use new types of legal form in line with a solidarity-based economy (Voss, *Wegweiser Solidarische Ökonomie).*

14 GA 189, p. 36, see also GA 328, p. 123.

15 Beck, *Volkswirtschaft verstehen.*

16 Herrmannstorfer, *Pseudo-Market Economy,* pp. 46ff.

17 In the journal *Sozialimpulse. Rundbrief Dreigliederung des sozialen Organismus,* No. 2/07, p. 8.

18 See www.sffo.de. The seminar's concept of land reform is published in 'Eigentum. Die Frage nach der Sozialbindung des Eigentums an Boden und Unternehmen,' *Sozialwissenschaftliches Forum,* Vol. 5, Stuttgart 2000. The same volume contains related essays by Jobst von Heynitz and Roland Geitmann.

19 Edith Maryon (1872–1924) was an English sculptor who collaborated closely with Rudolf Steiner in artistic and social fields. In 1919, the year it was first published, she translated into English the book now known as *Towards Social Renewal* (CW 23).

20 In the journal *Das Goetheanum,* No. 9/2008, pp. 8f.

4. Capital and the Means of Production

1 GA 331, p. 79.

2 GA 23, p. 106.

3 There are numerous examples of this, for instance, L'Aubier S.A. in Switzerland, described in Desaules, *A Human response to Globalisation.* See also Budd, *The Right On Corporation.*

4 GA 260a, lecture of March 29, 1924, p. 183.

5 GA 79, p. 246.

6 GA 341, p. 80.
7 GA 335, lecture of Sep 20, 1920, p. 267.
8 GA 329, pp. 20f.
9 GA 329, p. 33.

5. Sustainability and the Polarity of Agriculture and Industry

1 Stiglitz, *Making Globalization Work.*
2 Ruhland, *System der politischen Ökonomie,* Vol. 1, Chapter C, 2.
3 GA 337a, questions & answers after lecture of May 30, 1919, pp. 64ff.
4 Answering a question on Oct 29, 1919, Steiner spoke of 'how one should regard agrarian means of production, that is primarily the land and soil – for insofar as other means of production are involved, these are also industrial means of production ...' (GA 332a, p. 177).
5 See also Remer, *Laws of Life in Agriculture.*
6 GA 341, pp. 46f.

6. The Endeavour of Social Threefolding

1 In his lecture 'The Cardinal Question of Economic Life' of Nov 30, 1921, Steiner distinguishes 'three spheres of life in our social organism, which basically originate in three very different roots, and which are only connected in society through the individual human being.' (GA 79, p. 250.)
2 Lindenberg, *Rudolf Steiner,* pp. 655ff.
3 GA 332a, p. 104.
4 GA 330, p. 51.
5 GA 330, p. 54.
6 'Subsidiarity is an organizing principle of decentralization, stating that a matter ought to be handled by the smallest, lowest, or least centralized authority capable of addressing that matter effectively' (Wikipedia). This relates to what has been outlined above but is usually understood to mean higher and lower (subsidiary) orders. In the threefold social order, however, the state is not higher in status or power than the other two spheres.
7 CW 4.
8 GA 334, pp. 104f.

9 GA 186, Lecture of Dec 12, 1918 'Social and Antisocial Forces in the Human Being,' pp. 158ff.

10 GA 186, pp. 167ff.

11 GA 81, lecture of March 9, 1922, p. 116.

12 GA 341, pp. 87f. The 'interpreter' referred to was Professor Philipp Heck, with whom Steiner took issue in an essay of August 1919 (GA 24, pp. 434ff.). A recent book even refers to the idea of 'fourfolding'with four parliaments: Johannes Heinrichs, *Revolution der Demokratie, eine Realutopie,* Berlin 2003. Heinrichs initially agrees with Steiner, but then misinterprets the details of his ideas, and ends up passing very negative judgment on him. Compare my review of the book in the journal *Das Goetheanum,* Nos. 36 and 37, 2005.

13 GA 23, It is not easy to fulfil what Rudolf Steiner urged in 1919 in his preface to his fundamental book *Towards Social Renewal:* 'The ideas in this book have been drawn from an observation of life itself; an understanding of them can be derived from the same source.' p. 22.

14 CW 21, *Riddles of the Soul.*

15 GA 79, 'I call it associative action because, in associating in this way, the human individuality should be retained and safeguarded. This means that as we unite our powers with others, the individuality remains present. In coalitions and cooperatives the individuality is suppressed.' p. 263. This indicates that associations do not have the form of companies, and by no means are legal persons.

7. The Further Development of Democracy

1 Compare the thorough, carefully considered research by Eichholz, *Der Mensch im Recht.* He even said, 'Since external law has the task of making freedom possible, it must be retracted wherever possible', p. 63.

2 For this reason Eichholz said, 'The scope for shaping [of the law] is often greater than one supposes. In addition, it will not escape attentive scrutiny that there are hairline cracks in the system, where innovations can find a purchase. These are often only apparent to the professional, and require detailed knowledge of the particular field in question. Legal expertise is indispensable here.' p. 200.

3 The concept of a sense of justice indicates that the law as it stands develops through single cases. 'For the nature of feeling is the grasping of the moment; it lives in immediacy', Eichholz, p. 130.

4 GA 24, pp. 205ff.

5 GA 188, p. 243.

6 GA 186, pp. 100f.

7 GA 330, p. 278.

8 GA 331, p. 70.

9 GA 331, p. 64.

10 en.wikipedia.org/wiki/Government_spending.

11 Elisabeth Voss offers an interesting survey: *Wegweiser Solidarische Ökonomie.* The great number of examples shows that many people feel the need for a different kind of economy. Important anthroposophical instances can be found in Heisterkamp, *Kapital = Geist.* Felber, *Gemeinwohl Ökonomie* is a welcome book describing Common Welfare Economy. This demonstrates that individual companies can immediately embark on this kind of business, and will benefit from it. If they know of each other, in fact, they can favour each other as trading partners. The book recommends evaluating companies' social and ecological status by means of a points system. When shopping, everyone can note the companies that have a high score in this system, and alternative banks can favour such companies when giving credit. Felber emphasises that this economy is best developed not by prohibitions but by a system of stimulus and reward. The book includes a list of companies that first subscribed to the Common Welfare Economy principles. While there is overlap with threefolding, there are also important differences, yet it seems sensible to maintain contact with this movement and help to expand and develop it. www.gemeinwohl-oekonomie.org/en. en.wikipedia.org/wiki/Common_Welfare_Economy. en.wikipedia.org/wiki/Solidarity_economy

12 GA 331, p. 80.

13 GA 331, 'In future a certain concept will have to disappear entirely – the idea of the legal person and also of the economic legal person. The taxes that have to be paid will in fact be paid by individual human beings since in the state, the democratic state where justice should live, an individual human being faces another human being. People can only be equal where they meet one another as individuals.' p. 79.

14 GA 332a, 'In fully productive life, the sign of plentiful income is that one can spend a lot. Therefore, if we do not wish to create something in the tax system that feeds parasitically off the economic process but instead to create something that allows the economic process to serve the community, we must tax capital at the point where it is introduced into the economic process. Remarkably, it then becomes apparent that income tax has to be transformed into an expenditure tax – and please do not confuse this with indirect taxation. Indirect taxes nowadays often usually only surface when certain ruling powers are not obtaining as much as

they want from direct taxation, from income tax. I am not speaking either of direct or indirect taxation when I refer here to expenditure tax. Instead, at the moment where what I have earned passes into the economic process, where it becomes productive, also becoming subject to tax.', lecture of Oct 25, 1919, p. 61.

15 Hardorp, in *Arbeit und Kapital*, emphasises the advantages of VAT (sales tax) but seeks to use this to finance the state's greatly increasing social obligations, that is, for a 'basic income' for all, distributed by the state. This would give VAT the same properties Steiner criticised in indirect taxation. This is because a state distributed universal income would seek to enormously increase the state's tasks so that it intervened more than ever in the economy – in stark contrast to threefolding ideas.

16 GA 189, lecture of Feb 16, 1919, p. 33.

8. Economics and Law in the School Curriculum

1 GA 23, pp. 60f.
2 Public lecture in Zurich, Feb 25, 1919, GA 328, p. 123.
3 GA 294, pp. 161f.
4 GA 296, pp. 41f.
5 GA 296, p. 44.

Bibliography

Barkhoff, Wilhelm-Ernst, *Wir können lieben, wen wir wollen*, Stuttgart 1995.

Beck, Bernhard, *Volkswirtschaft verstehen*, Zurich 2005.

Binswanger, Hans Christoph, *Die Glaubensgemeinschaft der Ökonomen*, Munich 1998.

—, *Money and Magic: Critique of the Modern Economy in the Light of Goethe's 'Faust'*, Chicago 1994.

—, *Vorwärts zur Mässigung. Perspektive einer nachhaltigen Wirtschaft*, Hamburg 2010.

Blanc, Louis, *Organization of Labour*, Clarke, London 1848.

Brater, Michael & Claudia Munz, *Die pädagogische Bedeutung der Buchführung*, Stuttgart 1994.

Budd, Christopher Houghton, *Finance at the Threshold: Rethinking the Real and Financial Economies*, Gower Publishing, Farnham, Surrey 2011.

—, *Rare Albion: Further Adventures of the Wizard of Oz*, New Economy Publications, Canterbury 2005.

—, *The Right On Corporation: Transforming the Corporation, a micro response to a macro problem*, Canterbury 2004.

Desaules, Marc, *A Human Response to Globalisation*, Canterbury and Neuchatel 2004.

Dietz, Karl-Martin, *Dialogische Schulführung an Waldorfschulen. Spiritueller Individualismus als Sozialprinzip*, Heidelberg 2006.

—, *Produktivität und Empfänglichkeit. Das unbeachtete Prinzip des Geisteslebens*, Heidelberg 2008.

Eichholz, Reinald, *Der Mensch im Recht – das Recht im Menschen*, Basel 2011.

Felber, Christian, *Gemeinwohl Ökonomie, das Wirtschaftsmodell der Zukunft*, Vienna 2010.

Graeber, David, *Debt: The First 5000 Years*, Melville House, New York.

Hayek, Friedrich August von, *Denationalization of Money: An Analysis of the Theory and Practice of Concurrent Currencies* (Hobart Papers), Institute of Economic Affairs, 1977, also available in mises.org/books/denationalisation.pdf.

Gesell, Silvio, *Gesammelte Werke*, 18 vols., Luetjenburg 1991. English translation at: www.silvio gesell.de/neo_index1.htm.

—, *The Natural Economic Order*, rev. ed. Peter Owen, London 1958.

Greco, Thomas H. *Money and Debt: A Solution to the Global Crisis*, Knowledge Systems, USA 1990.

—, *New Money for Healthy Communities*, Greco, Tucson USA 1994.

—, *Money: Understanding and Creating Alternatives to Legal Tender*, Chelsea Green Publishing, USA 2001.

—, *The End of Money and the Future of Civilization*, Chelsea Green Publishing, USA 2009, and Floris Books, Edinburgh 2010.

Groh, Trauger & Steven McFadden, *Farms of Tomorrow Revisited: Community Supported Farms*, Biodynamic Farming & Gardening Ass., USA 2000, or from en.wikipedia.org/wiki/Community-supported_ agriculture.

Hardorp, Benediktus, *Arbeit und Kapital als schöpferische Kräfte. Einkommensbildung und Besteuerung als gesellschaftliches Teilungsverfahren*, Karlsruhe 2008.

Heinrichs, Johannes, *Revolution der Demokratie, eine Realutopie*, Berlin 2003.

Heisterkamp, Jens (ed.) *Kapital = Geist*, Info3, Frankfurt Main 2009.

Herrmannstorfer, Udo, *Pseudo Market: Economy, Labour, Land, Capital and the Globalisation of the Economy*, Biodynamic Farming & Gardening Ass., as pdf from www.threefolding.net.

—, *Scheinmarktwirtschaft. Die Unverkäuflichkeit von Arbeit, Boden und Kapital*, Stuttgart 1991.

Huber, Joseph, *Vollgeld*, Berlin 1998

Huber, Joseph & James Robertson, *Creating New Money. A monetary reform for the information age*, New Economics Foundation, London 2000 (also available at www.soziologie.uni-halle.de/huber/publikationen.html or www.jamesrobertson.com).

Kennedy, Margrit, Bernard Lietaer & John Rogers, *People Money: the Promise of Regional Currencies*, Triarchy Press, UK 2012.

Kerler, Rolf, *Eine Bank für den Menschen*, Dornach 2011.

Keynes, John Manyard, *Collected Writings*, Cambridge 1980.

Koepf, Herbert H. & Bodo Plato v. *Die biologisch-dynamische Wirtschaftsweise im 20. Jahrhundert*, Dornach 2001.

Lampe, Ernst Joachim (ed.) *Das sogenannte Rechtsgefühl*, Opladen 1985.

Lietaer, Bernard, *The Future of Money*, Random House, New York 1999.

—, *The Mystery of Money*, ebook 2000.

Lindenberg, Christoph, *Rudolf Steiner, eine Biographie*, Stuttgart 1997, English: *Rudolf Steiner, A Biography*, SteinerBooks, USA 2012.

Marx, Karl, *Critique of the Gotha Programme*, 1875.

North, Michael, *A Short History of Money*, Yale University Press 1959.

Remer, Nicolaus, *Sozialwissenschaft und soziale Praxis,* Verein für Forschung, Fortbildung und soziale Fürsorge auf dem Lande, Amelinghausen 2006.

—, *Laws of Life in Agriculture*, Rudolf Steiner Press 1995.

Riegel, E.C. *Flight from Inflation,* Los Angeles 1978, or www.newapproachtofreedom.info/documents/ffi.pdf

—, *The New Approach to Freedom, Together with Essays on the Separation of Money and State.* New York 1976, or monetaryfreedom.net/reinventingmoney/Riegel-New_Approach_to_Freedom.pdf and www.newapproachtofreedom.info/documents/naf.pdf

—, *Private Enterprise Money, a Non Political Money System*, New York 1944, or kentennant.com/rm/NAF/Documents/Enterprise.pdf.

Robertson, James, *Future Money: Breakdown or Breakthrough?* Green Books, 2012 (also from www.jamesrobertson.com).

Ruhland, Gustav, *System der politischen Ökonomie*, Berlin 1903–8.

Schmidt, Susanne, *Markt ohne Moral. Das Versagen der internationalen Finanzelite,* Knaur, Munich 2011.

Senf, Bernd, *Die blinden Flecken der Ökonomie*, DTV Munich, 2004.

Steiner, Rudolf. Volume Nos refer to the Collected Works (CW), or to the German Gesamtausgabe (GA).

—, CW 4, *Intuitive Thinking as a Spiritual Path: A Philosophy of Freedom,* Anthroposophic Press, USA 1995.

—, CW 21, *Riddles of the Soul*, Mercury Press, USA 1996.

—, GA 23, *Die Kernpunkte der sozialen Frage in den Lebensnotwendigkeiten der Gegenwart und Zukunft,* Dornach 1976. Various English translations: *Threefold Social Order,* Anthroposophic Press, USA 1966; *Towards Social Renewal: Basic Issues of the Social Question*, Rudolf Steiner Press, UK 1999; *Basic Issues of the Social Question,* ebook 2012.

—, GA 24, *Aufsätze über die Dreigliederung des sozialen Organismus und zur Zeitlage 1915–1921*, Dornach 1982. *The Renewal of the Social Organism,* Anthroposophic Press, USA 1985.

—, GA 34, *Lucifer-Gnosis: Grundlegende Aufsätze zur Anthroposophie,* Dornach 1987.

—, GA 54, *Die Welträtsel und die Anthroposophie,* Dornach 1983.

—, GA 56, *Die Erkenntnis der Seele und des Geistes,* Dornach 1985.

—, GA 79, *Die Wirklichkeit der höheren Welten*, Dornach 1988. *Self-Consciousness: the Spiritual Human Being,* SteinerBooks, USA 2010.

—, GA 81, *Erneuerungs-Impulse für Kultur und Wissenschaft*, Dornach 1994.

—, GA 158, *Der Zusammenhang des Menschen mit der elementarischen Welt,* Dornach 1993.

—, GA 186, *Die soziale Grundforderung unserer Zeit, in geänderter Zeitlage,*

Dornach 1990. (English translation of lecture of Dec 12, 1918: *Social and Antisocial Forces in the Human Being*, Mercury Press, USA 1982.)

—, GA 188, *Der Goetheanismus, ein Umwandlungsimpuls und Auferstehungsgedanke*, Dornach 1982.

—, GA 189, *Die soziale Frage als Bewusstseinsfrage*, Dornach 1980.

—, GA 190. *Vergangenheits- und Zukunftsimpulse im sozialen Geschehen*, Dornach 1980.

—, GA 192, *Soziales Verständnis aus geisteswissenschaftlichen Erkenntnis*, Dornach 1991.

—, CW 196, *Geistige und soziale Wandlungen in der Menschheitsentwicklung*, Dornach 1992. *What is Necessary in these Urgent Times*, SteinerBooks, USA 2010.

—, GA 260a, *Die Konstitution der Allgemeinen Anthroposophischen Gesellschaft*, Dornach 1987.

—, GA 294, *Erziehungskunst: Methodisch-Didaktisches*, Dornach 1990. *Practical Advice to Teachers*, Anthroposophic Press, USA 2000.

—, GA 296, *Die Erziehungsfrage als soziale Frage*, Dornach 1991. *Discussions with Teachers*, Anthroposophic Press, USA 1997.

—, GA 327, *Geisteswissenschaftliche Grundlagen zum Gedeihen der Landwirtschaft*, Dornach 1999. *Agriculture*, Biodynamic and Farming & Gardening Ass., USA 1993 (also www.rsarchive.org/Biodynamics); *Agriculture Course*, Rudolf Steiner Press, UK 2004.

—, GA 328, *Die soziale Frage*, Dornach 1977.

—, GA 329, *Die Befreiung des Menschenwesens als Grundlage für eine soziale Neugestaltung*, Dornach 1985.

—, GA 330, *Neugestaltung des sozialen Organismus*, Dornach 1983.

—, GA 331, *Betriebsräte und Sozialisierung*, Dornach 1989.

—, GA 332a, *Soziale Zukunft*, Dornach 2006. *The Social Future: Culture, Equality, and the Economy*, SteinerBooks, USA 2013.

—, GA 334, *Vom Einheitstaat zum dreigliedrigen sozialen Organismus*, Dornach 1983. *Social Issues: Meditative Thinking and the Threefold Social Order*, Anthroposophic Press, USA 1991.

—, GA 335, *Die Krisis der Gegenwart und der Weg des gesundem Denken*, Dornach 2005.

—, GA 337a, *Soziale Ideen, soziale Wirklichkeit, soziale Praxis*, Vol 1. Dornach 1999.

—, GA 337b, *Soziale Ideen, soziale Wirklichkeit, soziale Praxis*, Vol 2. Dornach 1999.

—, GA 339, *Anthroposophie, soziale Dreigliederung und Redekunst*, Dornach 1984. *Art of Lecturing*, Mercury Press, USA 1984.

—, GA 340, *Nationalökonomischer Kurs*, Dornach 2002. *World Economy*, Rudolf Steiner Press, UK 1973. *Economics: the World as One Economy*, New Economy

Publications, Canterbury 1996. CW340/341 *Rethinking Economics: Lectures and Seminars on World Economics*, SteinerBooks, USA 2013.

—, GA 341, *Nationalökonomisches Seminar: Aufgaben einer neuen Wirtschaftswissenschaft*, Dornach 1986. (English, see CW 340/341 above.)

—, GA 342, *Vorträge und Kurse über christlich-religöses Wirken*, Vol. 1. Dornach 1993. *First Steps in Christian Religious Renewal: Preparing the Ground for the Christian Community*, SteinerBooks, USA 2010.

Stiglitz, Joseph, *Making Globalization Work*, W.W. Norton & Company, New York 2006.

Voss, Elisabeth, *Wegweiser Solidarische Ökonomie. Anders wirtschaften ist möglich!* Neu-Ulm 2010.

Ziegler, Jean, *L'empire de la honte*, Paris 2001.

—, *La haine de l'Occident*, Paris 2008.

Index

INDEX

Graeber, David 16
grain money 47–49
Greco, Thomas H. 197–201
Groh, Trauger 98f
ground rent 62, 109–12, 118,
    120–23

Hasenmoor 101
Herrmannstorfer, Udo 41,
    116f

income 78
— distribution 89
—, personal 75f
— —, determining 86
industry 149, 151f
inflation 43f
interest 40–42, 190
—, compound 40
— rates 42
Islam 40

judges 77
Justinian, Emperor 175

Keynes, John Maynard 29
König, Karl 99

labour
—, income share of 62
— law 63–66
— market 67f
land 58, 60, 106
— administration 95f, 108
—, economic value of 109
— in public use 108
—, redemption of 119
—, value of 112–14
Langscheid, Christoph 119

law 173–75, 177
— codification 176
legal person 125–27
legal tender 22, 52
Lehmann, Christian 98
LETS (Local Exchange Trading
    Systems) 28, 198f
Lietaer, Bernard A. 28, 52, 202
loan money 18, 20, 32, 36f,
    43–45
location compensation fund 84
Loss, Carl-August 98

Machiavelli, Niccolò 174
market economics 69
market economy 60, 152
Marx, Karl 69
Midas, King 15
monetary reforms 51
monetative power (right to
    create money) 13
money
— creation 22, 24f
—, origin of 13f
— supply 49f
—, value of 46

needs economy 57

ownership 136–38

pensions 37, 122
price 58f
— index 47
production factors 57
production, primary 147, 150
production, refining 147, 150
profit 70, 73, 123
purchase money 18, 32f

220

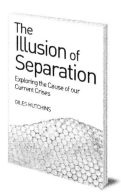

The Illusion of Separation

Exploring the Cause of our Current Crises

Giles Hutchins

`This is a well-expressed book on a fearfully important topic. Read it!'*
– Mary Midgley

Our modern patterns of thinking and learning are all based on observing a world of 'things', which we think of as separate building blocks. This worldview allows us to count and measure objects without their having any innate value; it provides neat definitions and a sense of control over life. However, this approach also sets humans apart from each other, and from nature.

In reality, in nature, everything is connected in a fluid, dynamic way. 'Separateness' is an illusion we have created – and is fast becoming a dangerous delusion infecting how we relate to business, politics, and other key areas of our daily reality.

Giles Hutchins argues that the source of our current social, economic and environmental issues springs from the misguided way we see and construct our world. With its roots in ancient wisdom, this insightful book sets out an accesssible, easy to follow exploration of the causes of our current crises, offering ways to rectify these issues at source and then pointing to a way ahead.

 Also available as an eBook

florisbooks.co.uk

Holonomics

Business Where People and Planet Matter

Simon Robinson &
Maria Moraes Robinson

'A powerful antidote to today's dominant culture'
– Fritjof Capra

Businesses around the world are facing rapidly changing economic and social situations. Business leaders and managers must be ready to respond and adapt in new, innovative ways.

The authors of this groundbreaking book argue that people in business must adopt a 'holonomic' way of thinking, a dynamic and authentic understanding of the relationships within a business system, and an appreciation of the whole. Complexity and chaos are not to be feared, but rather are the foundation of successful business structures and economics.

Holonomics presents a new world view where economics and ecology are in harmony. Using real-world case studies and practical exercises, the authors guide the reader in a new, holistic approach to business, towards a more sustainable future where both people and planet matter.

 Also available as an eBook

florisbooks.co.uk

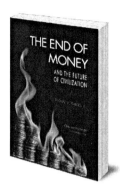

The End of Money and the Future of Civilisation

Thomas H. Greco

'*A refreshing read into the ails of the
current global financial system*'
– The Ecologist

Like the proverbial fish that doesn't know what water is, we swim in an economy built on money that few of us comprehend. And what we don't know is hurting us. *The End of Money and the Future of Civilization* demystifies the subjects of money, banking and finance by tracing historical landmarks and important evolutionary shifts that have changed the essential nature of money. Greco's masterful work lays out the problems and then looks to the future for the next stage in money's evolution that can liberate us from the current grip of centralized and politicized money power.

Greco provides specific design proposals and exchange-system architectures for local, regional, national, and global financial systems. He offers innovative strategies for their implementation and outlines actions that grassroots organizations, businesses, and governments will need to take to achieve success.

florisbooks.co.uk